Pirates of the Carolinas

Second Edition

Terrance Zepke

D0818510

Pineapple Press, Inc.
Sarasota, Florida

Inquiries should be addressed to:

Pineapple Press, Inc.
P.O. Box 3889
Sarasota, Florida 34230

www.pineapplepress.com

Library of Congress Cataloging-in-Publication Data

Zepke, Terrance.
  Pirates of the Carolinas / by Terrance Zepke.-- 2nd ed.
    p. cm.
  Includes bibliographical references and index.
  ISBN-13: 978-1-56164-344-8 (pbk. : alk. paper)
  ISBN-10: 1-56164-344-0 (pbk. : alk. paper)
  1. Pirates--North Carolina--Atlantic Coast--History. 2. Pirates--South Carolina-
-Atlantic Coast--History. 3. Pirates--North Carolina--Atlantic Coast--Biography.
4. Pirates--South Carolina--Atlantic Coast--Biography. 5. Atlantic Coast (N.C.)--
History, Naval. 6. Atlantic Coast (S.C.)--History, Naval. 7. North Carolina--History-
-Colonial period, ca. 1600-1775. 8. South Carolina--History--Colonial period, ca.
1600-1775. I. Title.
  F262.A84Z46 2005
  910.4'5--dc22
                                    2005017810

Second Edition
10 9 8 7 6 5 4

Printed in the United States of America

I would like to thank all those who gave their time and expertise to help me present an accurate account of Carolinas' pirates and the truth about piracy, especially the staff at the North Carolina State Archives; the Mariner's Museum at Newport News, Virginia; and David Moore at the North Carolina Maritime Museum.

Contents

Part II Pirate Lore and Resources

Introduction
Aye! To be a pirate!

Why was Blackbeard feared more than any other pirate? What was life really like for a pirate at sea? What was the typical booty (treasure)? Did Calico Jack leave his wife and crew to battle while he hid below deck? Did pirates force their victims to walk the plank? Did Anne Bonny actually become a pirate to avoid marrying a rich man her father had chosen for her? What did pirates eat during those long stints at sea? Did Mary Read pretend to be a male pirate by dressing up in men's clothes? Was Captain Kidd a privateer or an honest-to-goodness pirate? Did pirate Captain Henry Avery kidnap and marry the Great Mogul's daughter? What was the average life expectancy of a pirate?

Who were these men and women who chose to forsake everything to endure the harsh conditions of life at sea, endless skirmishes, and short lives that almost always ended in battle or at the gallows?

Remarkably, some were bored aristocrats, such as wealthy Barbadian plantation owner Stede Bonnet, and the infamous Captain Kidd. Female pirate Anne Bonny was the daughter of a prosperous Charleston businessman. But most pirates were uneducated men and women who were willing to do anything to escape eighteenth century social and economic restrictions. They took their chances and climbed aboard ships bound for places ranging from trade-heavy Asia to a growing colonial America. These sea robbers lived hard and fast, spending their riches as quickly as they could steal them, for they knew there were no guarantees of a tomorrow. Even if they weren't killed, life at sea was extremely difficult for pirates, and only the toughest survived.

Pirates' ships had big crews so they could overpower their opponents. Consequently, the men practically slept on top of one another, and there was seldom enough food to nourish them. It was nearly impossible to keep uncontaminated water for any period of time. Disease was prevalent because of unsanitary conditions and a lack of fruits and vegetables in the diet. Medicine to treat common ailments such as scurvy and malaria was more scarce than meat or a good night's sleep.

While many were willing to put up with all of this in the name of booty, finding capable men was difficult, so young, strong, healthy men were often shanghaied into service. Those forced into servitude didn't dare try to escape because a pirate captain rewarded such efforts with torture or left them marooned to die a lingering death on a deserted island. Life at sea was a like a pendulum, swinging from the high action and adventure of a good raid to deadly dull times of waiting for activity. Sometimes the pickings were slim, and pirates sat around with nothing to do but wait. Or weeks were spent doing hard labor in order to clean and recaulk a hull or repair sails after a storm or battle.

What most people don't realize is that piracy wasn't so much about getting rich as it was about having a way to live life on one's own terms. There wasn't another way to live so out of control on a daily basis than by piracy. Buccaneers could choose where they wanted to work, when they wanted to work, and how they wanted to work. A sea robber could spend months enjoying his share of plunder on a tropical island in the Caribbean. Then he could resume piracy and possibly recoup his money with a successful raid or two!

The life of these pirates has been examined in every medium, from the opera *Pirates of Penzance* to great literary works such as Robert Louis Stevenson's book *Treasure Island* and a lengthy poem, *The Corsair*, by English poet Lord Byron. Hollywood has produced its fair share of buccaneer films, ranging from *Captain Blood* to *Cutthroat Island*. During the 1950s, eight pirate movies were made in less than three years.

Why is it we remain so engaged by and curious about piracy? I think for most of us the fascination is not so much with the concept of piracy but rather with the personality of pirates. One had to be a certain kind of person not only to find this lifestyle appealing, but also to seek it with such reckless abandon–we can't help but want to know everything we can about these men and women.

The buccaneers chronicled in this book are some of the most engaging and colorful sea robbers in the history of piracy. Some were born in the Carolinas, some plundered its waters en route to other pirate havens, and some made their homes in numerous towns of North and South Carolina. They came from various backgrounds. Accordingly, these sea robbers all had different philosophies and idiosyncrasies. For instance, Blackbeard would do anything to protect and foster his reputation as the fiercest pirate of all. This behavior included putting lit fuses under his hat! William Lewis suppos-edly made a deal with the Devil and frequently conversed with him to become a pirate captain. Mary Read wanted so desperately to be a corsair that she taped her breasts and disguised herself as a man to join a crew.

The purpose of this book is to reveal the truth about piracy and the buccaneers who had a connection to the Carolinas. Thanks to booming port cities such as Charleston (formerly known as Charles Town, so named in honor of King Charles) and Beaufort as well as to the pirate-friendly governor of North Carolina, these states hosted many infamous pirates. North Carolina Governor Eden may even have performed Blackbeard's wedding ceremony!

To make this book as accurate as possible, I made numerous visits to maritime research facilities, the Library of Congress, the North Carolina State Archives, and the South Carolina State Archives, examining court transcripts and other written records that still exist. I also queried experts who have spent years researching these pirates.

Some aspects of a pirate's life we know about with certainty, such as death, trials, or pardons. Other things, such as why they behaved as they did, are only surmised. Buccaneers weren't much for record keeping. They barely maintained a ship's log and seldom wrote letters or kept a journal.

Perhaps by the time you have finished this book you'll be able to envision our coastal towns and waters as they were when pirates were a staple of the Carolinas. Certainly, you will have a better understanding of the personalities of these buccaneers and how they *really* lived and died.

The Pirate's Song

To the mast nail our flag; it is dark as the grave,
Or the death which it bears while it sweeps o'er the wave.
Let our deck clear for action, our guns be prepared,
Be the boarding-axe sharpen'd, the scimitar bared.
Set the canisters ready, and then bring to me
For the last of my duties, the powder-room key.
It shall never be lower'd, the black flag we bear,
If the sea is denied us, we'll sweep through the air.

Unshared have we left our victory's prey,
It is mine to divide it, and yours to obey.
There are shawls that might suit a sultanna's white neck
And pearls that are fair as the arms they will deck.

There are flasks which, unseal them, the air will disclose
Damieta's far summers, the home of the rose.
I claim not a portion: I ask but as mine–
'Tis to drink and our victory–one cup of red wine.

Some fight, 'tis for riches; some fight 'tis for fame:

This first I despise, and the last is a name.
I fight, 'tis for vengeance: I love to see flow,
At the stroke of my sabre, the life of my foe.
I strike for the memory of long-vanished years;
I only shed blood where another sheds tears.
I come as the lightening comes red from above,
O'er the race that I loathe to the battle I love.

Part 1

Gallery of Rogues

Blackbeard
Our Favorite Pirate

Records indicate that the buccaneer who later became the notorious Blackbeard began life with the name Edward Teach, or possibly Thatch. One source states that Drummond was his real name. Blackbeard's life came to an early end when he was killed in North Carolina during a battle with the Royal Navy. A shipwreck has been found near Beaufort Inlet, North Carolina, that is believed to be his main ship, *Queen Anne's Revenge*.

If this is Blackbeard's flagship, how did it end up here? According to some experts, it is believed *Queen Anne's Revenge* ran aground on a shoal during a trip the infamous pirate captain was making to Beaufort, and the ship was so laden

In spring 2005, the state of North Carolina initiated a program, Dive Down, which allows diving near the shipwreck popularly believed to be Blackbeard's flagship, *Queen Anne's Revenge*. The program allows up to 320 divers per year to participate in trips organized by dive shops. Officials are hoping that the supervised dives will help with public support for the ship–wreck project. Critics fear the access could lead to looting—just as Blackbeard himself might have done!

down that even the tide couldn't dislodge it. Subsequently, the ship got beaten up by the pounding waves of the tide, as well as by attempts to dislodge it. So, Blackbeard sent for another ship in his flotilla, *Adventure*, in hopes he could use the vessel to remove *Queen Anne's Revenge* from the shoal. Not only did the *Adventure* run aground on the same shoal, but *Queen Anne's Revenge* broke up from the abuse it had received. At this point, an agitated Blackbeard left both ships.

However, research has uncovered various letters and depositions that lend credence to the theory that the buccaneer ran both ships aground on purpose.

Regardless of which theory is correct, for roughly 280 years, the ships remained there. Until recently, no one searched for this vessel. However, Intersal, Inc., a commercial salvage company, has been working with the state of North Carolina (which is actually in charge of the excavation) on recovering artifacts since November 1996 when the team located a shipwreck near Beaufort Inlet (formerly Topsail Inlet).

According to all involved, it will take years to retrieve, conserve, interpret, and analyze the shipwreck and its artifacts. Meanwhile, the state of North Carolina is building a facility to study and display the artifacts. There was some discussion when the project first started concerning who would get the artifacts. Since that time, the North Carolina Maritime Museum has been named as the repository and primary curatorial facility.

As Blackbeard stood on deck preparing for his biggest battle, he did something that was highly uncharacteristic. He reflected on his life and events that led to this inevitable moment. He recalled his childhood, which took place in a southwest England town called Bristol. (Some accounts list London, Jamaica, even Philadelphia, as his home, but primary sources indicate he hailed from Bristol. Although some sources list his date of birth as 1675 or 1690, I am told by experts that these dates are pure speculation). By an early age he had become mesmerized by the sea, and couldn't stay away from the town's harbor, his only link to seafaring. The lad slipped off to sleep each night with dreams of great adventures and the thrill of life at sea.

His boyhood dream came true when he was granted the right to be a privateer sometime during Queen Anne's War against Spain, 1702-1713. (Although it is strongly suspected Blackbeard did serve as a privateer, there is no direct evidence of this belief). The line between being a pirate and being a privateer was a thin one, meaning the only thing that separated the two was a sheet of paper that bore the queen's signature. As a privateer, one had the right to attack enemy ships and seize their cargo, more popularly called "booty," in the name of the queen. A pirate had no such commission. Many privateers ultimately turned pirate or engaged in piracy for some period of time when there were no wars during which their services were needed by the Crown. Edward Teach was no exception.

By 1716, the privateer-turned-pirate had met up with another notorious buccaneer, Captain Benjamin Hornigold, in the Bahamas. The Bahamas were "pirate central," a safe haven and headquarters for sea robbers around the world. Pirates could be found all over the place, since Nassau on New Providence island had year-round sunny skies and balmy breezes, and was conveniently located on the European trade route. Hornigold and Teach took to each other immediately, and the young pirate eagerly signed on when Hornigold, who wanted the tough, rowdy pirate to join his crew, offered to teach him everything he knew. The first thing the elder pirate taught Teach, and perhaps the most significant lesson of all, was the importance of establishing a fierce, courageous image.

The youth was a quick study, and the two soon came to a new arrangement. Striking a deal as partners, the two men headed to America to try their luck. They met with much success in the waters around Delaware and Virginia. When the pair triumphantly charged a French slave ship, *Concorde*, off the island of St. Vincent on November 28, 1717, Teach asked Hornigold if he could have the ship. Hornigold, seeing the young man was anxious to command his own vessel, agreed. (Some documents indicate that Hornigold was not present when Blackbeard seized *Concorde*, but other records support the idea that he was still in charge, or at the very least sailing with Blackbeard in a "mentoring" capacity.) Soon after this, Hornigold accepted the king's pardon and retired from piracy. On the other hand, Teach assembled a crew, rechristened the 200-ton *Concorde* as *Queen Anne's Revenge*, and equipped it with forty cannons. He then set sail for the Caribbean, anticipating the many fruits of buccaneering that awaited him. The young pirate never forgot what he had been taught regarding image. To enhance his reputation as a savage and unmerciful sea robber, he grew a long, thick black beard, which he braided and tied off with ribbons. His new look earned him the name "Blackbeard." The combination of the beard with his coarse, wild black head of hair and massive mustache, gave the pirate nothing less than a sinister appearance.

In time, reports of successful assaults fueled the growing legend of Blackbeard to staggering levels. From port to port, he became known as the "Black-faced Devil" and the "Fury from Hell." The buccaneer carefully continued to cultivate this image.

Prior to battle he stuck slow-burning fuses up under his hat to hang down around his head. The fuses created a mystical smoke-haze that shrouded his face, a look that served to stun and intimidate his intended victims. It was no wonder mariners believed he was the devil himself! While many ruthless corsairs enjoyed torturing and murdering their victims, Blackbeard was nothing like them. He never harmed those on board, so long as they promptly surrendered. If they opted to battle it out, heaven help them! The pirate had a reputation to safeguard and would fight them to their expiration.

His former mentor and life at sea had taught Teach that sometimes pirates turned on their captains and took over the ship and crew. Determined this would never happen to him, Blackbeard sporadically took action to remind his men they'd better not dare. Once when the pirate leader, his trusted first mate, and another crew member were seated around a table in Teach's cabin drinking and socializing, Blackbeard quietly pulled a pistol from one of his numerous shoulder and waist gun slings and shot the first mate, Israel Hands, in the kneecap. As the injured man screamed in agony, he managed to cry out "Why?" to which Blackbeard laughingly bellowed, "If I don't kill somebody now and then, you'll forget who I am!"

Out of fondness for Hands, the pirate had made an example out of him by injuring the man, but not killing him. While the pistol ball in Hands' knee resulted in his being permanently crippled, Blackbeard kept him around anyway. The disabled man served as a continuous reminder to the crew of what could happen to them if they tried to best their leader. His men knew if Blackbeard would do such a thing to his trusted first mate, he wouldn't hesitate to harm or kill any other crew member.

The courageous seagoing swashbuckler did have one weakness-his love of women. Most pirates picked up prostitutes when they pulled into port, but not Blackbeard. He typically married the girls he wanted to be with, which explains why he had at least fourteen wives. Despite what the brides may have thought, these weren't real marriages. The pirate captain loved

A cannon was a large gun mounted on wheels. Loading and firing one took skill and discipline. Navy drill teams required a minimum of two to five minutes to get off a shot. Pirates, who weren't as well versed in cannon warfare, rarely got off more than one shot before having to continue battle using other weapons.

women, but had no intention of committing himself to any one woman. The shrewd seaman would bring his "beloved" aboard the ship and have the ceremony performed by a crew member! Brides weren't hard to find either, since there was no shortage of women who wanted to be with the nefarious Blackbeard. It seems the seaman was generous to his current "wife," and the matrimony was always a success until the pirate shipped out again and abandoned his bride.

Blackbeard continued plundering the waters of the Caribbean, where he met fellow pirate Stede Bonnet, and the two joined forces, with Blackbeard running the show. Bonnet had no problem with this arrangement, as he didn't particularly care about being in charge. Besides, he knew teaming up with the indomitable Blackbeard would ensure many prizes. The bold, cruel sea villain had little, if any, respect for Bonnet or his abilities as a pirate. The sole purpose Blackbeard had in joining up was to give himself an impressive flotilla. It was impressive with the forty-cannon *Queen Anne's Revenge*; Bonnet's ten-cannon sloop *Revenge*; the *Adventure*, an eight-cannon sloop that Blackbeard had claimed as prize from an assault that took place in the Bay of Honduras in April 1718; and a couple of small vessels, plus over three hundred men. The "Black-faced Devil" was often forced to attack vessels, not for any grand booty, but in hopes there was enough rum or ale in the hold to keep his many drink-loving men in line.

By 1718, Blackbeard had looted dozens of vessels, from Honduras to the coast of Virginia. Blackbeard terrorized the waters around St. Vincent, St. Lucia, Antigua, Puerto Rico, Hispaniola (Dominican Republic), Turneffe Islands (Bay of Honduras), Cuba, the Bahamas, and eventually America.

Perhaps that strenuous activity explains the pirate fleet's mysterious disappearance in early 1718, when Blackbeard, Bonnet, and their men dropped out of sight for most of January, February, and March. Possibly, all their hard work necessitated a good, long rest. Where they went or what they did will probably always remain a mystery, for records have not been discovered that would reveal this information. A rare, old book, *The Voyages of Edward Teach Commonly called Blackbeard* suggests the buccaneers were in the Grand Caymans during the three months in question.

One of Blackbeard's sloops, *Revenge,* under Lt. Richard's command, attempted to raid a heavily armed merchant ship, *Protestant Caesar.* Aboard the ship, Captain Wyar and his crew triumphantly held off the pirate attack. When Blackbeard heard of this, he was enraged by the defeat. He felt it reflected poorly on his hard-earned reputation. So Blackbeard set off in quest of the *Protestant Caesar.* He was obsessed with finding the ship and continued searching until he finally found it. When the crew saw Blackbeard's fleet coming straight for them, they quickly abandoned ship. He took all prizes found on board and burned the ship. Now satisfied his image would remain intact, he showed mercy and spared the lives of the crew.

Next, he committed his biggest and most outrageous act when he brought the city of Charleston (formerly Charles Town) to a standstill in May 1718 in what is known as "Blackbeard's Blockade of Charleston." Once he learned several noteworthy vessels were preparing to depart from the town's port, the pirate remained offshore at the mouth of the harbor and created a barrier that prevented these ships from getting past his fleet. Within a few days, he had captured eight merchant ships. One was a particularly big prize, the *Crowley,* since it had

May 1718: Governor Johnson to the Council of Trade and Plantations: "The unspeakable calamity this poor Province suffers from pyrats obliges me to inform your Lordships of it in order that his Majestie may know it and be induced to afford us the assistance of a frigate or two to cruse hereabouts upon them for we are continually alarmed and our ships taken to the utter ruin of our trade; twice since my coming here in 9 moneths time they lain off of our barr takeing and plundering all ships that either goe out or come in to this port, about 14 days ago 4 sail of them appeared in sight of the Town tooke our pilot boat and afterwards 8 or 9 sail wth. several of the best inhabitants of this place on board and then sent me word if I did not imediately send them a chest of medicines they would put every prisoner to death which for there sakes being complied with after plundering them all they had were sent ashore almost naked. This company is commanded by one Teach alias Blackbeard has a ship of 40 od guns under him and 3 sloopes tenders besides and are in all above 400 men. I don't perceive H.M. gracious proclamacon of pardon works any good efect upon them, some few indeed surrender and take a certificate of there so doing and then severall of them return to the sport again. . . . This company is commanded by one Teach alias Blackbeard has a ship of 40 od[d] guns under him and 3 sloopes tenders besides and are in all above 400 men. . . . " *(Letter from Gov. Johnson, South Carolina, June 18, 1718, CSPCS Vol. 30, #556)* many prominent citizens on board, including a member of the Council for Governor of South Carolina, a Mr. Samuel Wragg. He sent one of the passengers, Mr. Marks, accompanied by two of Blackbeard's men, to South Carolina Governor Johnson to disclose Blackbeard's demand, which was a chest of medicine. Blackbeard also issued a warning that if the medicine wasn't promptly delivered, he would kill those he held captive, as well as destroy the city of Charleston. Experts speculated that Blackbeard raided these ships to obtain a "retirement fund" before giving up piracy.

While the hostages and residents held their breath hoping for the best and anticipating the worst, the threesome took the captain's demands to the governor. The time allotted by the pirate captain to meet his demands came and went. Blackbeard grew agitated and impatient. As he stood on deck contemplating the attack on Charleston, a rowboat carrying a lone fisherman appeared. As the man pulled up to the ship, he nervously began explaining that the boat that was taking the three men to the governor had overturned during a storm and that they were forced to obtain another vessel. He said he had been hired by Mr. Marks to bring word of this delay to Blackbeard.

Upon learning this, the hostages pleaded with Blackbeard to be patient a while longer, but the sea robber wasn't accustomed to waiting, nor was he very good at it. He felt sufficient time had passed for the men to have returned, even with the delay. At that moment, Blackbeard's two men could be seen rowing as fast as they were able towards the ship. As they got within shouting distance of Blackbeard, they told their leader that it had taken some time to get all the medicine he demanded. What the men didn't tell him was that once all the medicine had been secured, the two pirates had fled. The governor, however, had authorized a thorough search of the town, knowing that if Blackbeard's men didn't return with the medicine, the sea captain would think they had been imprisoned and would probably annihilate Charleston anyway. Finally, searchers found the scoundrels getting drunk in a pub.

No one knows why the buccaneer wanted the medicine so desperately that he was willing to take on an entire town. It's believed many of his men were sick with disease and battle wounds that couldn't be tended to with the medical supplies the ship's doctor had on hand. It's also thought that Blackbeard needed medicine because he had caught syphilis from one of his "wives"! Once Blackbeard had the medications in his possession, he released his hold on Charleston and set his prisoners free, but not before making off with the cargo from each ship he had temporarily snared, which included about £1,500 in gold and silver coins. That would have been a substantial retirement fund in 1718! Experts remain perplexed as to why Blackbeard didn't ask for money in addition to the medicine chest when he held Charleston hostage.

Blackbeard headed for North Carolina in June 1718, where he felt confident he could obtain a pardon for this heinous act. He was sure Governor Eden would grant him one because trade-poor North Carolina still welcomed rogues such as himself. And he was right. Since North Carolina had no cash crops, the pirates were too good for the economy to be turned away. The buccaneers sold their ill-gotten goods at a deep discount to the citizens, while they, in turn, sold their goods and services to the pirates. What the pirate didn't realize was that the recent attack on Charleston was the last straw for those fed up with piracy. South Carolina Governor Johnson, as well as Virginia Governor Spotswood, was sick of this kind of tyranny, and they determined that, whatever the cost, they would put an end to the likes of Blackbeard. But the "Fury from Hell" wasn't concerned about them; he had more pressing problems that required his immediate attention.

Now that he wasn't cruising the open seas, Blackbeard decided his crew was too big. The booty was unnecessarily being split many ways. *How shall I eliminate some of them?* he wondered. The sea robber particularly wanted to be rid of Bonnet. While the dapper, inept pirate had amused Blackbeard for a while, it had never been his intent for this to be a permanent arrangement.

The cunning pirate sailed the flotilla into Topsail Inlet and then deliberately ran *Queen Anne's Revenge* and *Adventure* aground. (While there is strong evidence to support this, there is no way of knowing for sure whether Blackbeard did indeed run aground on purpose.) Next, Blackbeard sent Bonnet and some of his men ashore on the pretense of checking on the pardon and obtaining some provisions. Immediately after their departure, the ruthless pirate had his men strip the *Revenge* of all of its provisions and booty and load it all onto the smaller, sleeker *Adventure*. (This was not the same *Adventure* that he grounded, but another sloop. Names such as *Revenge* and *Adventure* were common for pirate ships). Blackbeard chose to get rid of the bigger vessels because he needed one more suitable for maneuvering the shallow waters and islands of the Carolinas.

The pardon that Blackbeard sought was called "The Act of Grace," which was extended by North Carolina Governor Charles Eden by the authority of King George of England. The king had extended a "Proclamation for Suppressing of Pyrates." This applied to English privateers who committed acts of piracy after Queen Anne's War, which started in 1702 and ended on June 24, 1714. The Act of Grace went into effect on September 5, 1717, and was good for one year, although at least one extension was given.

Next, he marooned around eighteen men on a sandbar on his way to Bath. The pirate captain now had "40 whites and 60 negroes." Some experts believe the majority of these blacks were actually slaves that Blackbeard intended to sell or trade.

. . . . .

When Blackbeard reached Bath (formerly Bath Town), North Carolina, in June 1718, he learned his pardon had been granted by Governor Charles Eden of North Carolina. Although it has never been proven, it is believed the two worked out an arrangement whereby the pirate would share any "findings" with the governor. They became business cohorts and friends.

According to legend, a tunnel that ran from Bath Town Creek to the basement of Governor Eden's house was used for the purpose of smuggling stolen goods. It is unknown whether Eden built the structure or whether it already existed when he bought the property. There is some evidence that Blackbeard lived on a farm outside Bath, and the governor's home was reportedly situated between the home of Customs Collector Tobias Knight and Blackbeard's home. While there is no proof of a business relationship between these men, there are documented eyewitness accounts indicating that a tunnel did indeed extend from the creek to Governor Eden's house. It was described as "...a Subterranean passage some 60 or more yards in length, communicated from a brick wall near the margin of the creek, with the cellar of the dwelling." Governor Eden got rid of the 400-acre plantation and acquired another property when gossip began to link him to illicit activities and the "smuggler's tunnel." There are no records indicating whether Eden bought the property, and if so, from whom and for how much. This omission is deemed odd by historians who wonder if it means that Eden wanted that information kept confidential. Documents do show that Eden sold the plantation in April 1718 to John Lillington.

Allegedly, the governor performed Blackbeard's wedding ceremony to a planter's daughter, once the girl finally agreed to marry him. Legend has it she was betrothed to another, but

Blackbeard ultimately got his way when he swore to give up piracy for good. This sacrifice didn't bother the buccaneer because once he saw the beautiful, sixteen-year-old Mary Ormond, Blackbeard fell in love for the first time in his life and wanted her at any cost.

Convincing both himself and his bride that he could give up piracy, he settled down in the small community of Bath, where he became somewhat of a local celebrity. For a while Blackbeard was happy with this life and his true love, but then he began to miss the excitement of his former life.

He established a headquarters for a small smuggling operation on one of North Carolina's remote Outer Banks barrier islands, Ocracoke Island, in hopes that smuggling would fill his growing void. Unfortunately, being a pirate wasn't a mere livelihood to Blackbeard, it was a lifestyle that was as essential to him as the blood that coursed through his veins.

Blackbeard gave it his best effort, but by fall of that same year, he headed north to resume piracy. He had to change his plans when he discovered Pennsylvania Governor Keith had issued an arrest warrant once he learned Blackbeard was in the state. The adaptable pirate captain quickly changed his scheme and headed to Bermuda.

En route, Blackbeard couldn't resist seizing two French merchant ships out of Martinique. A search of their holds showed both vessels were carrying sugar and cocoa. Knowing the revenue these scarce items would bring in North Carolina, Blackbeard had the sugar and cocoa transferred to one ship, which he sailed to Ocracoke. He put all the French crew onto the other merchant ship and sent them on their way home.

Upon arriving at North Carolina, he told Governor Eden and the Bath Customs Collector Tobias Knight the story he had concocted. The corsair claimed he had found the ship deserted! Eden and Knight, realizing the value of the large amounts of cocoa and sugar, were eager to believe this story. They declared the ship a derelict, and the three split the booty. Fearful someone might recognize it and contradict Blackbeard's tale, the pirate set fire to the ship.

Nonetheless, word reached Virginia Governor Spotswood of Blackbeard's deed. The governor then declared any pardon given to Blackbeard to be null and void in light of this recent act. Spotswood began a crusade that originated with his hatred of piracy but turned into a desperate effort to save his waning political career. Spotswood believed that if he could get rid of Blackbeard, he would be a hero and his career would be saved. The desperate politician sent word of Blackbeard's latest villainous deed to London, hoping for support from the Royal Navy.

All the while, notorious pirates such as Calico Jack Rackham and Charles Vane began arriving at Ocracoke Island. It soon became the site of a huge, continual party that has also been described as the "Ocracoke Orgy." For one week, the biggest gathering of pirates on the entire eastern seaboard took place at Ocracoke Island. Good food, lots of drink, and anything else desired was plentiful. Wild and wicked sea villains chased women around the beach, while musicians played all night.

A good time was had by all until one by one the pirates sailed off, ready to get back to work. Blackbeard, however, was having so much fun he was reluctant to stop. He stayed at Ocracoke, oblivious to the hysteria his fellow seamen's presence had created. Panic spread that Ocracoke was to be the new pirate headquarters, replacing former safe havens Madagascar and the Bahamas.

Apparently no one took into consideration that all the pirates but Blackbeard had left, or perhaps the citizens didn't want to take any chances that the marauders might return to the place where they had been shown such a good time. The residents were growing very tired of Blackbeard's actions. For some time he had been assaulting merchant ships without consequence, thanks to Governor Eden.

•　•　•　•　•

Virginia Governor Alexander Spotswood got the support he

needed from the Royal Navy and was finally able to take action. (It's believed that His Majesty King George, who ascended the throne upon the death of Queen Anne in 1713, didn't know anything about the planned assault until after the fact.) Captains Gordon (HMS *Pearl*) and Brand (HMS *Lyme*), by virtue of their commissions, had the authority to approve Spotswood's plan. The men agreed that if Spotswood supplied the ships, England would provide the military manpower, spearheaded by Lieutenant Maynard.

Governor Spotswood's mission was in clear violation of "The Act of Grace," whereby Blackbeard received his pardon. While it may have been suspected that Blackbeard was up to no good, there was no proof of piracy against him. This is the very reason why so many pirates were leery about accepting a pardon. Many who did so were later jailed.

Spotswood subsequently obtained two suitable vessels (the *Jane* and the *Ranger*) but didn't divulge his plan to his constituents because he was sure his methods would not be approved, and he was also afraid someone might leak word to the nefarious Blackbeard. But before Spotswood and Maynard could activate their scheme, they had to pinpoint where the clever pirate's hideout, Teach's Hole, was located. It was known that Blackbeard and his cronies were in the area, but it wasn't known just where in the labyrinth of channels and inlets he

> **Blackbeard may have had a sister who lived on a plantation on Beard's Creek (named after Captain James Beard, not Blackbeard), which flowed into the Neuse River (Craven Co.). Her name was Susie or Susannah, and legend has it that whenever the pirate visited his sister, he posted a lookout in a tree that afforded panoramic views. Blackbeard did not like surprises, especially unwanted visitors!**

was enjoying himself. This problem was nicely solved when Blackbeard's quartermaster was arrested and coerced to reveal how many men Blackbeard currently had with him and where the hideout was located.

Lieutenant Maynard, like Governor Spotswood, was also anxious for this attack to be successful in order to jolt his career out of its stagnation. He was the oldest lieutenant in the Royal Navy. Capturing Blackbeard would be a huge feather in his cap, guaranteeing recognition and a much-needed promotion. With the promise of a one-hundred-pound reward if Blackbeard was brought in dead or alive, Maynard secretly set off with the *Ranger* and the *Jane* and fifty-eight able men.

The two sloops were loaded with axes (used to board an enemy ship), as well as muskets, pistols, and cutlasses. There were no cannons on either vessel, so they would be light enough to enter the shallow waters where Blackbeard was hiding. Although Maynard and his men arrived by dusk, they had to wait until dawn to navigate the treacherous shoals. What a long night that must have been for Maynard!

At daybreak on November 22, 1718, the two navy vessels pulled up their anchors and entered the inlet. It is hard to believe, but proof exists that Blackbeard had knowledge of this supposed ambush. First, Tobias Knight, Customs Collector of Bath, had learned that an assault of some sort was being planned on Blackbeard, and he sent the pirate a warning note.

At any rate, the pirate would easily have been able to see the navy ships' masts as the sloops sluggishly maneuvered the inlet. Why didn't Blackbeard take the opportunity to escape, which he could easily have done by slipping through the inlets and channels that he knew so well? He didn't even have all his men aboard the *Adventure*, so he had to have known that he would be at a disadvantage. Indeed, Maynard's men outnumbered Blackbeard's almost three to one. It seems Blackbeard had fallen victim to believing his own public relations story that he was invincible, that he was the Devil himself!

As Maynard got closer, the pirate cut his sloop's anchor and headed towards Ocracoke Island. The battle was on! During this chase, a famous exchange of words took place between the two determined men.

Blackbeard shouted, "Damn you for villains, who are you? And whence came you?"

"You may see by our colors we are no pirates."

"Send your boat alongside mine so I can see who you are."

"I cannot spare my boat, but I will come aboard of you as soon as I can with my sloop," Lieutenant Maynard answered.

Knowing that Maynard was saying that he meant to forcibly board Blackbeard's vessel, the pirate grabbed a glass of rum and toasted Maynard, saying, "Damnation seize my soul if I give you quarters, or take any from you."

"I expect none, nor shall I give any."

Maynard continued his pursuit, unaware that this chase was all part of Blackbeard's plan. The pirate captain intended to ground Maynard's ships on the sandbars that surrounded the island, rendering them powerless against an attack. Both of Maynard's vessels did run aground, and Blackbeard seized the opportunity to launch a full scale assault on the *Jane*. The resourceful pirate had his men load their guns and cannons with iron bars and spikes, which splintered the wooden mast and ripped the sails to shreds. The sloop was disabled, its captain killed, and most of the crew injured or dead. Before Blackbeard could give his full attention to the other enemy vessel, the winds abruptly changed and his sloop also went aground on a sandbar.

While Blackbeard and his men were busy trying to push their sloop from the sandbar, Maynard got the *Jane* off the sandbars by lightening its load. He accomplished this by dumping the ballast and water barrels overboard. Maynard continued the battle with only his ship and surviving men. The navy lieutenant figured thirty well-trained and armed military men against twenty-three pirates suffering hangovers was hardly a match.

As the Royal Navy *Jane* pulled up next to the *Adventure*, Blackbeard counter-attacked by throwing hand grenades onto

Grenades were made using a mixture of tar and rags, which were stuffed into a small clay-type bottle and then lit. Reportedly, the grenades used by Blackbeard were empty glass bottles filled with black powder and shrapnel.

its deck. When the smoke cleared, no one was left standing on deck but Maynard. All Blackbeard saw was mangled bodies littering the deck. Believing all the men had been seriously wounded or killed, the irate sea bandit jumped on board to finish off the man who had disturbed his revelry and challenged his reputation.

Now Maynard had the pirate right where he wanted him. The navy officer knew he had to get Blackbeard and his men onto the *Jane.* If they boarded the navy vessel, Maynard would have the advantage of not having to board and attack the pirate's ship. The lieutenant's deceit worked! The shrewd sea dog fell for his trick.

As soon as Blackbeard's boots hit the deck, the military men come up from below deck, where Maynard had ordered them to hide when Blackbeard started throwing the grenades. When Blackbeard's crew saw the peril their leader was in, they immediately leaped aboard the navy sloop to help him. This ten-minute showdown between Maynard and Blackbeard and their men is recorded as one of the "bloodiest battles that ever took place," because the bloodshed from the numerous wounded and dead bodies rapidly painted the deck a dark and gory red.

Maynard and Blackbeard both fired off shots at each other. The pirate's shot missed, but Maynard's hit the pirate in the shoulder. Blackbeard barely flinched at the gun wound as he seized his cutlass. Maynard also grabbed his, but it broke at the first cross. He then whipped out a pistol and again shot the buccaneer, but the man who had earned the reputation "Black-faced Devil" refused to die. Instead, he again swung his cutlass.

He was about to kill the navy officer when one of Maynard's men came up behind him and struck him so viciously with a cutlass that he nearly detached Blackbeard's head from his shoulders.

Lieutenant Maynard took advantage of this attack to get off another shot at the pirate, but the indomitable sea robber didn't give in to death until he had suffered five pistol wounds and over twenty cutlass wounds. When the pirate's crew saw their leader finally collapse and die, they abruptly stopped fighting and surrendered. The gory conflict resulted in ten dead pirates, including Blackbeard, plus nine wounded. Maynard also lost ten men, and twenty-four suffered injuries.

Meanwhile, a man in the hold of the *Adventure* set about laying a trail of gunpowder across the floor to the ammunitions chest. As he was about to light the gunpowder, another man jumped him and they began scuffling. The commotion brought Maynard and his men below deck to find out what was going on. It seems Blackbeard had thought of everything. He had commanded one of his most trusted crew members, a giant black man named Caesar, to stay in the hold during the aggression. If it seemed as if Blackbeard wasn't going to win, Caesar had been instructed to blow up the *Adventure*, thereby killing the navy men as punishment, and killing the pirates so they would avoid prosecution. When a prisoner realized what Caesar intended to do, he attacked him to keep him from his assigned duty.

When Maynard climbed back up on deck, he examined Blackbeard's corpse and finished chopping off its head. He then threw the body overboard and hung the head from the bowsprit as they made their way back to Virginia. The pirate's head served as more than a trophy, it also showed he had done the job. This proof was necessary if he was to collect the promised reward from Governor Spotswood.

. . . . .

The buccaneer's death resulted in litigation between Governors

A 1733 map indicates "Thatches Hole" at Ocracoke. This later became known as "Teach's Hole." None of this provides definitive proof as to who Black-beard really was because he could have used an alias. Pirates commonly used aliases rather than their real names for fear of reprisals. The only thing that is certain about Blackbeard's identity is that he was not a descendent of a prominent South Carolina family, Drum-mond—that theory has emphatically been disproved.

Eden and Spotswood because Maynard found a letter aboard the *Adventure* that was signed "T.K.," which was thought to be Tobias Knight, the customs collector. The letter from Knight to Blackbeard was addressed "Captain Edward Thache." The letter showed that Knight had contracted with the pirates to raid ware-houses holding sugar, cocoa, indigo, cotton, and other booty, which he and the pirates then shared. Governor Eden avoided any court action because of Knight's popularity and influential friends. Knight was acquitted by the North Carolina Council of any wrongdoing but died before any further action could be taken by Virginia.

The sale of the confiscated goods were part of Maynard and his men's reward, although they did not receive it for nearly four years. The pirates who surrendered after watching their leader die were also taken to Williamsburg, Virginia, where they were tried on March 12, 1719, and all but two were subsequently hanged. Blackbeard's shipmaster and former captain Israel Hands received a king's pardon just one day before his scheduled execution. He lived his remaining years as a beggar. Another crew member, Samuel Odel, was acquitted. Odel reportedly received seventy wounds during battle, but survived!

And so one of the greatest pirates of all time and Black-beard's Two-Year Reign of Terror in the Carolinas came to an end. Or did it? Legend has it that when Blackbeard's corpse was thrown overboard, it swam around the vessel several times. The pirate, still unwilling to accept death, may have been looking for his head. Or it may be that he was waiting to make sure his orders to blow up the *Adventure* were carried out.

More about Blackbeard

Unanswered Questions

It is reported that Blackbeard captured more than fifty ships and had a crew of up to four hundred men at the height of his "career." There is also a story about a man who was robbed by Blackbeard on the Pamlico River in 1718. When the startled fellow asked the buccaneer where he came from, Blackbeard replied, "From Hell." Many of our questions regarding Black-beard would be answered if his logbook and other pertinent papers could be found. Unfortunately, Lieutenant Maynard took all of the pirate's papers back to Virginia with him, and it is not known what ultimately happened to them. Some copies of letters and documents were sent back to North Carolina, but most disappeared. Even the trial records of the surviving pirates of that final, bloody battle have not been found. There was a fire in the Virginia records office in 1740, which may have destroyed the documents. They could have also ended up in England (although there has been an exhaustive search there, as well) or in a private collection.

North Carolina Division of Cultural Resources

Archives and History has established a website on the excavation of what is believed to be Blackbeard's ship. The site includes an excavation assessment plan, FAQ's, and video footage. "Investigating N.C. Shipwreck 0003 BUI: Queen Anne's Revenge" http://www.ah.dcr.state.nc.us/qar/

A website has been created for those pirate enthusiasts who want to follow the exploits of Blackbeard and learn about the excavation of what is believed to be his ship.

Note: There are a few experts that dispute this is Blackbeard's flagship. However, those working on the QAR project say the group's contradictory conclusions are based on "early research and misinterpreted reports." They are also quick to point out that no definitive evidence may ever be found, only circumstantial evidence.

•   •   •   •   •

Not a Killer?

Despite Blackbeard's fierce and ruthless reputation, the sea robber may not have killed anyone until his final battle. There is no proof that Blackbeard ever killed anyone. This could certainly be true since most captains immediately surrendered when they saw Blackbeard's flag.

•   •   •   •   •

Facts About Queen Anne's Revenge

- Christened the *Concorde*, it was a French slave ship (1713) before Blackbeard and Hornigold captured it in 1717.

- Blackbeard renamed the vessel *Queen Anne's Revenge*. The ship was 80 to 90 feet long, 24.5 feet wide, and had a carrying capacity of 200 to 300 tons. It served as Blackbeard's flagship until it ran aground in June 1718.

- The ship's galley was located well away from any ammunition or powder. It probably contained a brick stove that had built-in kettles.

. . . . .

Blackbeard, the Womanizer

During Blackbeard's time in Bath, North Carolina, it is written that he and his cohorts took liberties with wives and daughters of the same planters who invited him to dinners and parties. If these husbands and fathers only knew what he whispered to the young ladies as he dined or danced with them!

Although it is rumored that the nefarious pirate married thirteen or fourteen times, these were almost assuredly "mock weddings." The ladies may have presumed the ceremonies were real, but the clergyman was most likely one of Blackbeard's crew, acting the part of a clergyman. Blackbeard may have actually gotten married on a couple of occasions: to Mary Ormond and to the daughter of his neighbor, Thomas Worsely. It is even alleged that he dated Governor Eden's daughter, Penelope, but the governor probably wasn't interested in having a pirate for a son-in-law!

. . . . .

Blackbeard's Home

The town of Bath was formed in 1705 on the shore of the Pamlico Sound. Bath was the state's first town and an official port for clearing customs. In 1785, the county government moved to Washington. When that happened, the town "dried up." During Blackbeard's era, more than five thousand people resided here. Today, it has fewer than five hundred residents. Still, town inhabitants remain proud of their former celebrity resident–three historic markers highlight his time in Bath, including Plum Point, which is about a mile south of Bath across the creek. An old pier and rotting foundation are all that's left of what is believed to have been the pirate's home at one time. Across the creek were Governor Eden and Customs Collector Knight's residences. The land surrounding Bath Creek has been developed and one of them is aptly named Black-beard's View.

. . . . .

Could it be?

When Blackbeard's men were captured, several claimed that there were times while they were at sea that a man was sometimes seen, on and below deck–a man who was not a crew member. By the time they realized no one knew who he was, the man had vanished! The pirate crew adamantly swore it was the Devil himself, keeping an eye on his protégé, Blackbeard.

. . . . .

Blackbeard's Deal with the Devil

Blackbeard once proclaimed no one, save the Devil and himself, knew where he had secured his booty. Whoever lived longer would get all the riches. "Teach's Lights" are part of a legend about this. It is said that on clear nights the waters around Teach's Hole, Ocracoke Island, possess a unique shine and glimmer. This is when Blackbeard swims these waters in search of his head, which was chopped off during a battle with the Royal Navy. Supposedly, anyone who follows these lights will eventually find Blackbeard's treasure, and the Devil himself will be seated on top of the chest, waiting to receive his promised booty.

* * * * *

The Skull Cup of Blackbeard

This is the strangest and most fascinating folklore regarding Blackbeard. When Lt. Maynard brought the buccaneer's head back to Virginia, it was suspended from a pole at the harbor in Hampton, Virginia. Legend has it the skull eventually turned up in some secret "bones society" at Yale University. This is disputed by some who claim Blackbeard's friends stole the skull off the pole. It's also believed the skull once belonged to one of the fraternities at William and Mary College. The skull ended up in North Carolina, supposedly, in the possession of an anonymous businessman. At some point, the skull was covered or plated with silver.

It's believed that during the time it was in this man's possession, former North Carolina judge, legislator, and author, Charles H. Whedbee, drank from the skull, also referred to as "Blackbeard's Cup," sometime in the 1930s. An anonymous group arranged a secret rendezvous, which reportedly took place at "Blackbeard's Castle," a nickname given to the pirate captain's former refuge house on Ockracoke Island, near Silver Lake. Sadly, Whedbee is deceased, the house no longer exists, and no one has any idea who the other people in this group were, assuming this event took place, so no further information can be obtained.

The silver-plated skull came to belong to Edward Rowe Snow in 1949, who was also fascinated with piracy. After his death, his widow gave the skull to the Peabody Essex Museum in Salem, Massachusetts. It was on exhibit at the Mariner's Museum in Newport News, Virginia in 1996, and the Peabody put it on exhibit for five months in 1998. Peabody Museum Assistant Curator Lyles Forbes told me it is not really silver-plated, just painted silver. Also, the lower jaw is missing, most likely a casualty resulting from age and rough handling. Forbes says it will never be possible to prove or disprove that the skull is Blackbeard's.

•　•　•　•　•

The Legend of Blackbeard's Revenge

During one of his many visits to Bath, North Carolina, Blackbeard glimpsed a girl whose beauty was so overwhelming he thought the rum he was consuming must have caused hallucinations. The pirate carried on with his merriment and forgot about the girl, until he chanced upon her again.

She had long, curly hair that fell gently across her shoulders and flowed down her back. As if the shiny, thick curls didn't enhance her enough, she had vivid blue eyes that were so compelling he almost missed her perfect lips. He figured they were as soft as her flawless, pale complexion. Although a connoisseur of women, Blackbeard had never been so affected as he was by this one. Blackbeard decided right then and there he must have this girl at any cost. He sent for her, only to be rewarded with a polite rejection.

"While I am flattered at your attentions sir, I am sure I cannot receive them for I belong to another. I am engaged to be married in a fortnight. Best Wishes, Mary."

Furious beyond comprehension, he had the girl brought to his room. As she stood in front of the tall swarthy pirate, he gave her another chance to change her mind. She said she loved the man she was engaged to and looked forward to their nuptials. The pirate seemed to take her words well, and began issuing orders and making preparations to set sail. Foolishly, the girl took that to be the end of the matter.

Later that day a spectacular engraved gold-and-wooden box arrived at her home. When she opened it she screamed in horror, for it contained a human finger! A note was next to it informing her that was all she'd ever see again of her fiancé, and it was signed by the pirate. The buccaneer didn't lie. The young man Mary was to marry was never seen again.

The pirate knew what he was doing. He knew she would suffer more if he let her live and instead killed the man she loved. The beautiful girl went to pieces, unable to get past the guilt she felt for her fiancé's death. Fishermen and sea captains, once even a boat full of passengers on a dinner cruise, say they have seen a woman fitting this description down by the docks on the anniversary of the day the couple were to be married.

An even more astonishing end to this tale, if it is true, is that the young lady Blackbeard wanted so badly was Mary Ormond, who finally did agree to his proposal once he consented to give up piracy.

Unfortunately, the buccaneer wasn't able to keep his word, returning to the seas and his old ways before long. The young bride used to linger at the docks, waiting for Blackbeard to return.

The next three chapters are devoted to Anne Bonny, Jack Rackham, and Mary Read. Despite their diverse backgrounds, the trio ended up united throughout most of their adult lives. Anne Bonny and Mary Read hold a place in history as two of the most famous female pirates ever, while Jack Rackham earns a spot for his unique style and association with these women.

ANNE BONNY
Wild, Reckless, and Gallant Pirate

Anne Bonny, the most famous and fascinating female pirate, was never able to deny her passions. She did whatever she pleased and took whatever she wanted.

Her life began in Cork, Ireland, circa 1697-1705, as a consequence of attorney William Cormac's affair with the family maid, Peg Brennan. There's a strange story in one account of Anne Bonny's life as to how this affair became known. It seems a servant stole some spoons, and the maid told him to put them back or she would tell who had taken them. As a joke, he returned them but not to the kitchen. Instead, he placed them under the maid's pillows for her to find when she went to sleep. The next day Mrs. Cormac told Peg she would have to sleep with the other servants since Mrs. Cormac needed the maid's room. Her mother-in-law was coming to visit and would be staying in Mrs. Cormac's bedroom, so she would be sleeping in Peg's bedroom.

That night, as she slipped into her maid's bed, she discovered the missing spoons under her pillow. As she was pondering this, a bigger deception was revealed. The door opened and a male figure made its way through the darkness towards the bed. Just as she was about to scream, the woman heard a familiar voice whispering, *"Peg! Peg!"* It was her husband!

After this incident, the truth was slowly divulged. The servant admitted his part in pilfering the spoons. His story further incriminated Cormac and Brennan since the spoons would have been found the day before if the maid had slept in her own bed the previous night! Also, it was soon apparent that Peg Brennan was pregnant, and there was little doubt as to the father. From here, accounts vary as to whether William Cormac blatantly continued a relationship with the maid, miscalculating the impact it would have, or whether gossip was the reason it became public knowledge. It doesn't really matter which was the case because the end result was the same. When it became known who the father of this illegitimate baby was, that was the end of William Cormac's marriage and his successful law practice.

He made the decision to leave Ireland and go to America. William Cormac took what money he had, along with his mistress and baby daughter Anne, and boarded a ship bound for Charleston (formerly known as Charles Town in honor of King Charles), South Carolina. It turned out to be a good decision on his part. In time, he became a prosperous lawyer, merchant, and plantation owner. However, he was not as triumphant at fatherhood, and things only got worse when Peg Brennan died of typhoid fever just after Anne's thirteenth birthday. Cormac did the best he could, but besides having insufficient parenting skills, he was consumed with his growing law practice and enormous plantation, so he just couldn't give Anne the attention she needed.

And Anne needed a great deal of attention. Anne was high-spirited, to say the least. She also delighted in dressing and acting like a boy. The rebellious teen was good at shooting, hunting, riding, and even cursing! Despite her minimum efforts with her appearance, this tomboy was stunningly attractive. Anne had the smooth porcelain skin of the Irish, as well as a beautiful head of thick, red curly hair she refused to tie up, so it draped her face and shoulders like a lion's mane. A story in *The Pirates' Own Book*, 1837, reports that Anne once attacked a young man who tried to have his way with her. She assaulted him so violently that he was bedridden for weeks.

Although the girl had many eligible men trying to court her, she was not interested in settling down. By the time she was nineteen, William Cormac took matters into his own hands and arranged for her to marry a prominent member of the community. For a young woman who didn't want to answer to anyone and longed for great adventure and excitement, this prospect must have seemed like a lifelong prison sentence. Unable to bear the thought of having to stay in Charleston betrothed to this stolid fellow her father had chosen for her, she eloped with a young sailor she'd been seeing on the sly, James Bonny. The union was definitely more about freedom than true love. Anne saw the sailor as her way out of the restrictive social setting of Charleston, and as an opportunity to see the world on her own terms.

Unfortunately, Anne quickly became bored with her husband. They ended up in New Providence where her husband became an informer for Governor Woodes Rogers. Anne came to despise her husband for his "snitching," and she had begun pursuing other options when she was seen by pirate Jack Rackham in Nassau on New Providence. He was there in hopes of obtaining the king's pardon, but got distracted from his mission when he saw Anne Bonny. The instant he laid eyes on the wild redheaded woman, "Calico Jack" Rackham fell head over heels in love. His feelings were reciprocated by Anne. For the first time in her life, Anne Bonny discovered the real meaning of love.

Rackham tried to get Anne's husband to divorce her by offering him a large sum of money, but James Bonny refused the money and proclaimed he would never let his wife go. He even went as far as revealing Anne's infidelity to the governor. Under the governor's threat of official recrimination for their adulterous actions, Anne and Calico Jack stole a ship, assembled a crew, and set sail, not telling anyone their destination.

• • • • •

Anne probably found further excitement in the charade of having to conceal her identity by dressing as a man, since women weren't allowed to crew or even be aboard pirate ships. More importantly, it would have diminished Rackham's authority if he had blatantly brought a woman on as part of the crew. It probably wasn't as difficult as one might think to pull off this sham—the clothes were loose fitting, and boys were employed as powder monkeys. Without make-up and with her hair put up under a hat, Anne could have passed for one of these lads without close scrutiny.

Powder monkeys were the boys who loaded the gunpowder into the cannons and large guns.

●　●　●　●　●

The pair continued the deception for months. During this time, they managed to successfully assault and raid some small merchant vessels. However, in 1720 something happened that nearly ended their relationship. Rackham overtook a Dutch merchant ship, captured the crew, and forced them into servitude. Anne Bonny began spending a great deal of time with one of the new pirates. Calico Jack often spotted them huddled together, whispering.

Jealousy besieged Rackham. In a rage, he confronted Anne and the English pirate, promising to kill both for their indiscretions. Anne was forced to tell Calico Jack the truth. She divulged that the man he thought she was carrying on with was nothing more than a friend, a very good friend. Anne then formally introduced her new best friend. "Jack, I'd like you to meet Miss Mary Read!"

Shortly after this, the women abandoned their disguises, but not the manly clothing. Having proven themselves to be more adept than most male pirates, their revelation was well received. But, just as they were accepted as female buccaneers, Anne found out she was pregnant and had to be taken to Cuba to have the baby.

As Nassau, Bahamas, was to partying pirates, Cuba was to pirate families. It was a safe haven where women raised the children while the men remained pirates, returning when- ever they could.

If Calico Jack hinted that Anne could stay in Cuba to raise the child, Anne must have quickly told him otherwise, for she was back on board within a few weeks. The baby was most likely stillborn or given to another pirate family to raise. All that was important to Anne was the freedom of being a pirate because it was a great outlet for her untamed spirit. It was one of her happiest days when she was once again part of Captain Jack Rackham's pirate crew. Little did she or any of them know that the high times they had shared were behind them. Soon after Anne's return, their ship was attacked while docked at Point Negril, Jamaica. The assault was led by British Captain Barnet, who had been sent by the Jamaican government as part of the new crackdown on piracy.

Rackham and his crew were so drunk that they could not defend themselves. In fact, some had already passed out from their over-consumption. The remaining crew, including Captain Rackham, hid in the cargo hold during the attack. Only two pirates, Mary Read and Anne Bonny, stayed and fought. Despite the calls and challenges of both women for the pirates to come up and fight, the men stayed below deck. The pair reportedly fought well but were over-matched and ultimately taken as prisoners. All the pirates were taken to Port Royal, Jamaica to be tried.

There was an interesting turn of events at their trial. Captain Jack Rackham was found guilty and sentenced to be hanged, which didn't seem to upset Anne Bonny at all. Mary Read's lover was acquitted when he proved Calico Jack had forced him into piracy. And Mary Read and Anne Bonny both announced they were pregnant. An examination by a doctor revealed this to be true, so both were spared execution.

In early 1721, Anne Bonny was sent back to Charleston, South Carolina. One engaging theory is that her influential father had the doctor paid off to falsely report Anne was pregnant so she would not be hanged. We know she never returned to piracy, but what happened to her remains unclear. Regardless of how she lived her remaining years, it's safe to assume she must have longed for her bygone days on the open sea where her restless, troubled spirit had briefly found a home.

· · · · ·

Hollywood made a film about the life of Anne Bonny in 1951. Unfortunately, *Anne of the Indies* was more fiction and exaggeration than truth.

· · · · ·

According to legend, Anne used to help her father run his enormous plantation by taking charge of the kitchen help. There was a servant girl that Anne didn't like. The feeling was mutual and the slave was slow to carry out Anne's demands. Some accounts credit her father, William Cormac, with being the real source of contention. Had history repeated itself? Was Cormac having an affair with this young woman just as he had with Anne's mother? Apparently, Anne believed so and killed the servant girl one afternoon in a fit of anger.

John "Calico Jack" Rackham

He was nicknamed Calico Jack because his clothes were all derived from a type of cotton known as calico. He also wore bright, festive colors, which was uncommon for pirates.

John Rackham was the first mate of the infamous pirate Captain Charles Vane. After a successful raid on a merchant vessel, the *Kingston*, Captain Vane put Rackham in charge of the newly obtained ship. Not long after this, Vane refused to attack a ship, despite being urged on by his men. Declaring him a coward, they voted to replace Vane with Rackham. The new pirate captain put his former boss, along with Vane's loyal followers, aboard a smaller sloop and assumed command of the crew and ship.

Shortly after this incident, war broke out between England and Spain. Rackham decided to get a king's pardon and take up the lucrative life of a privateer. It was while he was in New Providence awaiting word on his pardon that he met Anne Bonny. As soon as he saw Anne he wanted her. He plied the beautiful young woman with sweet talk and extravagant gifts. When she became receptive to his attention, Rackham tried to get her husband, James Bonny, to grant her a divorce. But, the former sailor turned pirate-informant would not hear of it. Instead, he sought retribution for his wife's adulterous actions from the governor. As was the law at that time, she was sentenced to a public flogging for betraying her husband. (This law, however, did not apply to a man who had an affair).

The lovers quickly assembled an eight-man crew and "selected" the boat they wanted, which was a pirate-outfitted sloop. While its captain, John Haman, was away from the vessel, Anne used her feminine wiles to find out how many men slept aboard and where. The night before Anne was to be collected for her beating, the duo and their newly formed crew stole the ship. Rackham put ashore the two guards Captain Haman kept on the ship and set sail for the Caribbean. He renamed the ship the *Curlew*, and unbeknownst to the other sea robbers, a disguised Anne Bonny was also aboard.

Among their successful assaults was the overtaking of a Dutch merchant ship. The pirates captured the crew and forced them into servitude. Captain Rackham noticed Anne Bonny was spending a great deal of time with one of the new pirates. In a fit of jealously, he threatened to kill the pirate. In order to prevent this, Anne was forced to tell Calico Jack the truth. The pirate was her new friend, Mary Read. Rackham was so relieved that Anne was not having an affair that he didn't even care he had been outwitted. He may have cared more if the entire story had been told–that Anne had originally been interested in starting an affair with someone.

. . . . .

Anne became pregnant, and Rackham took her to Cuba to have the baby. During her absence, Rackham and his crew stayed in the West Indies from November 1718 until early 1719. The pirates then headed to

Anne had expressed a strong romantic interest in the attractive pirate. It was only at that point she discovered Mary Read was also a woman. Soon after this, the women revealed their true identities to the crew and were accepted as female pirates.

Bermuda, where they seized New England and North Carolina trade ships, before returning to the Bahamas. Woodes Rogers, governor of the Bahamas, heard of Rackham's presence, and as part of his crackdown on piracy, set out to capture him. He snatched up two prize sloops Calico Jack had brought from Bermuda, but the buccaneer and his men managed to escape.

By now it was time to collect Anne. Off the island of Cuba, a Spanish man-of-war blocked the *Curlew* in a channel. Knowing the pirate was cornered, the Spanish captain decided it would be best to wait until the following morning to attack.

Again Rackham and his group narrowly escaped. During the night, Rackham put his crew onto one of his small boats and lowered it into the water. The men quietly rowed away to the other side of the island. There, the lucky leader found an English ship anchored. He and his crew took it by cutting its cable and easing it out to sea, threatening to kill its crew if any of them uttered a single word. In the morning, the Spanish warship assaulted Rackham's abandoned ship and battled it for some time before they realized no one was aboard!

Deciding it was becoming too dangerous to be a pirate around the Indies, they headed to North Carolina where it was well known that Governor Eden not only tolerated pirates but welcomed them. However, before long the buccaneers ended up back in the waters around Jamaica. Although it is not known why they left the Carolinas, most likely it was for the same reason they left the Indies. South Carolina Governor Johnson and Virginia Governor Spotswood were capturing pirates right and left. Many of the pirates' sea-robbing friends had already been killed or executed, including the legendary Blackbeard.

Rackham and his crew needed provisions, and they had always done well around Jamaica, so they headed there. Upon arrival, they began attacking ships around Jamaica and captured a sloop that had been raided by pirates only a couple of months before. This was considered the final straw by the governor of Jamaica, who sent British Captain Jonathan Barnet after this pesky pirate. Meanwhile, the *Curlew* was tied up off Point Negril, Jamaica. Rackham and his men had been celebrating, and most of them were passed out or too drunk to stand when they were attacked by Barnet.

It came down to the two female pirates, Mary Read and Anne Bonny, as well as Captain Rackham and another crew member, to save them all. The next thing the women knew, Rackham and the other pirate had abandoned them, opting instead to join the men already below deck! The women tried to get them to come back and fight. The females yelled insults and even shot into the hold, but the men did nothing. Eventually, the women were forced to surrender and they were all taken to St. Jago de la Vega, Jamaica for trial. During the proceedings, Calico Jack Rackham was found guilty.

On November 17, 1720, he was hanged at Gallows Point, Port Royal, Jamaica. The former lovers were allowed one last visit before his execution. Whatever Rackham expected of Anne, it was not the cold, unsympathetic words she gave him, ". . . if you had stayed and fought like a man, you need not be hanged like a dog."

Mary Read

This English woman led a normal life until her husband died. Then, forsaking everything to fill the void in her heart, she took to the sea.

Mary's mother was married to a sailor who disappeared at sea before the birth of their son. After the loss of her husband, the woman had the baby and began seeing another man, who abandoned her once he learned she was pregnant with her second child. Soon after Mary's birth, the baby boy died. Dire poverty necessitated a deception the woman maintained throughout Mary's childhood. The destitute mother dressed

There were no physicals for those entering the military in the 1700s. As a matter of fact, a doctor never even saw a recruit. The young man enlisted and was given an assignment, as well as one month's pay. Like pirates, servicemen didn't bathe often. And not even members of the same sex undressed in front of each other in those days as it was considered a sin.

Mary in boy's clothes in an effort to substitute the little girl for the deceased boy, so her mother-in-law would contribute money to sustain them. The charade was necessary because the mother-in-law would have never given money to take care of the illegitimate child.

By the time Mary Read was a teenager, she abandoned femininity for the advantages granted to those of the male persuasion. At age thirteen or fourteen she got a job as a pageboy for a French woman. She quickly tired of the position and opted instead to bind her breasts to disguise her sex and enlist in the military.

• • • • •

The young woman served as a cadet in the British Army. There she learned everything about battle, stamina, and bravery she would ever need to know. Mary also grew discouraged because, despite her ability, she could not get a commission (become an officer). The promotions were not based on merit, but were purchased. Because of Mary's background and lack of education, she would never have been sold a commission, even if she could have afforded to buy one.

During her time with the army, she fell in love with another soldier. After she disclosed her real identity to him, he came to love her also. The pair told a shocked troop this secret, and their captain arranged honorable discharges for both of them. The lovers were subsequently married. Mary Read wore a dress, for the first and perhaps only time in her life, at her wedding. The entire company contributed money towards the future of the well-liked couple.

With that seed money, the newlyweds opened a tavern, The Three Horseshoes, near Castle of Breda in Brabant, Holland. The drinking establishment supplied a good income, and the couple was very happy until tragedy struck. Her husband died of fever, leaving Mary with a tremendous void in her life. Another strike against the young widow was the recent peace treaty. The pact ended the need for officers in the area, thereby eliminating most of the pub's patrons. A combination of the floundering business and the emotional emptiness created by her husband's death resulted in Mary's decision to return to the military. However, Mary soon left the service as the excitement she longed for was nonexistent in peacetime.

The young woman signed on with a Dutch merchant ship en route to the West Indies. The vessel was overtaken by sea villains, and the pirate captain forced her to join his crew. For Mary, this turned out to be the biggest and best adventure she had ever undertaken. However, in 1718, Mary Read and fellow pirates accepted the king's pardon (brought to Nassau by the governor of New Providence in the Bahamas, Woodes Rogers). But money ran low, and Mary grew extremely bored with civilian life. In the fall of 1718, the twenty-something-year-old heard that Woodes Rogers was looking for priva-teers, and so she signed on with a privateering vessel. Before long, this ship was taken over by Calico Jack Rackham, and once again Mary was forced into piracy.

Little did Mary Read know she was not the only female pirate on board. Anne Bonny was still disguising her real identity. Not knowing about each other, the two women began to spend a great deal of time together. As their friend-

> **There was a die-hard rule that pirates could not fight among themselves at sea. This was to prevent the crew from taking sides and engaging in a free-for-all.**

ship grew, Anne Bonny realized she was attracted to Mary Read. She made her interest known when she showed her breasts. Much to Anne's shock, Mary Read disclosed she was a woman, too! Promising to keep each other's secret, they became best friends. Shortly after this, Jack Rackham threatened to kill Read. He had watched the two closely and firmly believed they were lovers. He was madly in love with Anne Bonny and was determined no one else, let alone a member of his crew, would have her. Anne kept him from doing Mary any harm by blurting out Mary's secret.

A triumphant attack on a ship resulted in Rackham's taking more seamen into servitude. One of them was an Englishman named Tom Deane. Deane and Read soon became lovers. Although the pair never officially married, she considered him her legitimate husband. He was a likable fellow, and all of the crew was fond of him, with the exception of one pirate. He needled the young man at every chance. Finally, unable to endure anymore, Deane challenged his tormentor to a duel. The match was set for the next day when they would reach land.

• • • • •

Mary knew she had to do something. Her sweet, lovable man was no match for the colossal, fierce pirate he had challenged. Tom Deane was a navigator and had barely even picked up a gun, much less a sword. A few hours before the scheduled duel, Mary went up to the brute and began plying him with insults until he challenged Mary to a duel. She eagerly accepted, and both Mary and her opponent were armed with a cutlass and a pistol. Mary easily won the duel, killing her adversary. Soon after this, both Anne Bonny and Mary Read abandoned their disguises. By this time, the crew was so impressed with their abilities that they didn't object to their being female pirates.

The Jamaican prisons were some of the worst in the world, with conditions beyond deplorable. Very few prisoners survived if they received lengthy sentences.

The corsairs briefly plundered the Indies and America before returning to Jamaica. They frequented the island of Hispaniola and the north coast of Jamaica, specifically Porto Maria Bay. During the early fall of 1720, Rackham, Read, Bonny, and the rest of the pirate crew continued their sea robbing, but with little to show for their efforts. They captured a few fishing boats and Jamaican sloops, which gave them only tobacco, tackle, and food provisions.

In November 1720, their ship was attacked by a military vessel. It was led by Captain Johnathan Barnet, who had been sent by the governor of Jamaica, Sir Nicholos Lawes. Taken by surprise, the crew was not prepared to do battle. Most were too drunk to stand, let alone fight. In fact, many were passed out and couldn't be awakened. Only Mary Read and Anne Bonny stayed and fought. Everyone else, including Captain Jack Rackham, hid below deck. As the women realized they were going to lose the battle, Mary raised the lid to the hold and furiously fired her pistols into the darkness. Her action wounded one man and killed another.

The pirates were taken prisoner, and the trial was speedy.

Mary Read and Anne Bonny, among others, were found guilty of piracy. Both pleaded extenuating circumstances: "My Lord, we plead our bellies." A doctor's examination confirmed their claims. Since they were pregnant, both women were sentenced to prison but not executed. Mary Read became ill with fever and died in a Jamaican jail in 1721. Her lover, Tom Deane, convinced the court he had been coerced into service and was one of the few men released.

William Fly

What happened to William Fly serves as proof of why pirates could never trust another living soul.

Little is known about this pirate except that he came from Jamaica and had little education but great ambition. Supposedly, Fly had been a prizefighter but gave it up when he learned of the riches pirates achieved. The buccaneer was hired as a boatswain by James Green, commander of the *Elizabeth*, in April 1726. Green didn't know he had employed a pirate, but this was revealed en route to their destination, Guinea, when Fly led the crew in a mutiny.

The captain was awakened from a drunken slumber and

informed he could go up on deck willingly, or not, as a few buckets of water would surely take his blood out of the floor-boards. Despite Green's pleas, Fly did not give the captain a chance to crew for him or allow him to be put ashore. He also ignored Green's insistence that he was not ready to stand in judgment before God since he had not yet confessed his sins. Instead of giving him opportunity to do so, the pirate callously flung the former commander into the sea.

Remarkably, instead of going overboard, Green grabbed the mainsail and managed to hang onto it. To get the man to let go of the sail, one of Fly's cohorts chopped off Green's hand with an ax, which resulted in ear-splitting screams as the man plunged into the sea.

Green's loyal first mate, Thomas Jenkins, was also dragged onto the deck. He fought so hard that he made the pirates who were in charge of him angry, and they tried to cut off his head. Because Jenkins was struggling heavily, they missed and instead cut a hunk out of his shoulder. Next, the former first mate was thrown overboard to face the same monstrous drowning death as Green. After they disposed of the two men, a big batch of liquor punch was made and a party commenced to celebrate William Fly's new command.

Fly ended up in waters off the coast of North Carolina where he seized many ships, the first of which was the *John and Hannah*. The newly elected captain assaulted the ship while it was stuck on a sandbar. The sea villain never showed mercy to the captains or crew of captured vessels. In fact, he seemed to delight in torturing the men.

Fly told the captain of the *John and Hannah* to get the vessel off the sandbar. When Captain Fuller reported that the ship's bilge had been ejected to float her but that she had sunk from efforts to comply with Fly's orders, the buccaneer became furious. He forced Captain Fuller to strip and subjected him to a tremendous beating. He then kept him prisoner.

Fly soon found another victim, a merchant ship bound for Guinea from Barbados, called the *John and Betty*. Ordinarily, Captain Gale would have surrendered since he currently had nothing of value aboard his vessel. But, he had heard horror stories of what Fly did to his victims, so he fled. Fly pursued him for hours and hours until he was close enough to use his guns. Gale did his best but ultimately had to surrender. Remarkably, Fly released Gale and most of his crew, keeping only the best men.

One of these men was an excellent pilot, and the sea marauder needed a skilled pilot to get to New England. It's unclear why he left the waters of the Carolinas. A great many things have been surmised, such as that Fly had heard there were bigger prizes up north. He may have just wanted a change of scenery. Pirates never stayed in any one place very long. Whatever the reason, Fly went to New England.

Atkinson was no pirate, but he was smart enough to recognize that he had better ingratiate himself with the crew. In time, the men grew to like and trust the pilot. They especially liked the caricatures he drew for them. Every time the suspicious pirate captain suggested throwing Atkinson overboard, the crew came to his defense. In time, even the pirate captain became less cautious with him. This was to be William Fly's downfall.

Atkinson, along with some other men who had been forced into servitude, came up with a plan that they put into action when Fly captured a ship near Nantucket. Fly planned to use a sloop as a ruse for getting merchant ships close enough to plunder. He put most of his men on this vessel, leaving only himself, a few pirates, Atkinson, and Atkinson's schemers aboard the pirate ship. The crafty pilot knew this was the moment. He nodded to his cohorts and they seized Fly and his pirates, keeping them prisoner. The group quickly distanced themselves from Fly's other ship and horde of pirates. The new leader brought the ship to Boston and turned in the captive sea robbers.

The trial was held on July 4, 1726 at the Boston court-house. William Fly's brief career as a pirate was over. The Honorable William Dummer, Esq., lieutenant governor and commander in chief of the providence of Massachusetts Bay and president of the Special Court of Admiralty, assisted by eighteen councilmen, found William Fly and his men guilty of murder and piracy. William Fly, Samuel Cole, George Condick, and Henry Greenvil were executed on July 12, 1726, and their tarred bodies hung for a while near Boston Harbor for all to see.

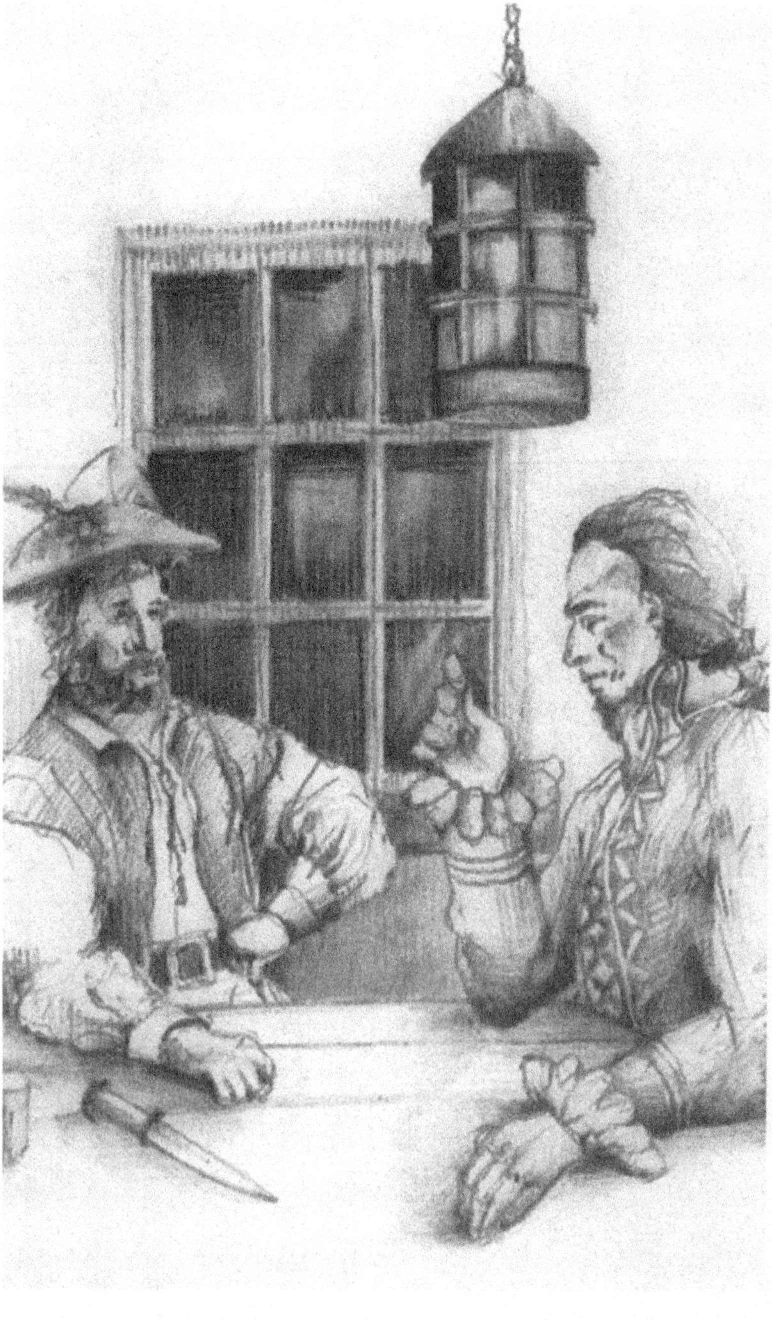

Henry "Long Ben" Avery

Henry Avery became so illustrious that he was known as the "Arch Pirate" and "King of the Pirates." Henry Avery was also called Long Ben Avery because he was so tall.

Avery was born in Devonshire, England, which is near Plymouth. During his childhood, his father tried to make him scholarly, but Henry Avery was wild and uninterested in academics. The youth ran away to sea, where he was such a troublesome boy that the captain kept him locked in the hold until he reached Carolina. (Since historical records only indicate "Carolina" we don't know whether this was North or South Carolina).

At this point he had the young man put off the ship. Three years later, a merchant vessel returned him home. Avery's father died while he was away, and soon after the youth's return, his mother died. Her death was attributed to the strain of her husband's death and her missing son.

The youth was then placed under the guardianship of a local merchant, Mr. Lightfoot. Before long, the businessman went bankrupt and Avery was again on his own. The boy took to stealing to survive, but went back to sea when he was about to be caught.

As a young man, Avery secured the position of first mate aboard a privateering ship, *Duke*, under Captain Gibson's command. The clever and ambitious Avery instigated a revolt and took over the ship when he was twenty years old.

The captain had passed out from too much "punch." When he awoke and felt the ship moving, he rang Avery and demanded an explanation. Their conversation, reported in Captain Johnson's *A General History of Pirates*, went like this:

> [Avery replied,] "We're at Sea, with a fair Wind & good Weather."
>
> "At sea! How can that be?" asked Captain Gibson.
>
> "Come", says Avery, "don't be in a Fright, but put on your cloathes, and I'll le[t] you into a Secret: You must know that I am Captain of this Shipe now, and this is my Cabin, therefore you must walk out; I am bound to Madagascar, with a Design of making my own Fortune, and that of all the brave Fellows joined with me."

The former captain and those loyal to him were put out in a boat to make their way to shore. Captain Avery renamed the vessel *Fancy*, then sailed to a favorite pirate spot, Madagascar, where he posted a letter to the attention of all English commanders:

> I was riding her in the *Fancy*, man-of-war, formerly the *Charles* of the Spanish expedition...being then and now a ship of 46 guns, 150 men, and bound to seek our fortunes. I have never yet wronged any English or Dutch, nor ever intend whilst I am commander...If you or any whom you may inform are desirous to know what we are at a distance, then make your ancient [ensign] up in a ball or bundle and hoist him at the mizen peak, the mizen being furled. I shall answer with the same, and never molest you, but my men are hungry, stout, and resolute, and should they exceed my desire I cannot help myself...
>
> As yet an Englishman's friend
> –Henry Avery

The main point of the correspondence was to warn everyone that there was a new and powerful pirate on the loose. The underlying message was obvious. Merchant ships would be wise to surrender their riches immediately rather than try to escape or retaliate. How well received this warning was would soon be revealed.

Avery sailed with two pirate sloops led by Captains Tew and Mission, who had joined up with him. They took prizes and added more men to their crew in Madagascar, the West Indies, Newfoundland, and the Arabian Coast.

In September 1695, the trio chased, attacked, and captured the chief vessel of the Indian Mogul's fleet, *Gang-i-Sawai*, in the Gulf of Aden at the mouth of the Red Sea. The ship contained six hundred passengers, many of them high officials of the Mogul's court, as well as ladies of the court, slave girls, attendants, and concubines. They were on a pilgrimage to the Muslim holy city of Mecca, and so they had offerings to present at the Shrine of Mahomet (Mohammed).

· · · · ·

The "Arch Pirate" Avery and his men gave no leniency since the captain and passengers did not heed the advice circulated in his letter. What the pirates did was wicked and unnatural to any sane person. The Indian crew were mutilated and tossed overboard to the sharks. The Indian captain had hidden the girls and women below deck when the pirates gave chase, and had ordered them to dress like men. After the brutal and bloody battle, the pirate captain ordered all the passengers strip-searched to ensure that they were hiding no valuables. When it was discovered they were women, the pirate crew went wild, raping and ravishing all those who hadn't committed suicide.

· · · · ·

Many of the girls and women were taken aboard the *Fancy* as amusement for the crew, but as the men grew bored with them, they flung them into the sea. It was a long crossing, and the females probably took up too much precious space. Besides, pirates aren't known for their long attention spans.

Avery convinced the two other pirate captains that their loot would be safest aboard the *Fancy*–if there was trouble, the *Fancy* was the fastest sloop and most capable of escape. During the night while the other pirates were passed out from their drunken celebration, Captain Long Ben Avery and his men quietly took off with all the riches–plunder worth £325,000 (which would be equivalent to around $400 million today). Each crew member received £2,000 (around $2.5 million in today's value).

. . . . .

Many of the ladies of the high court killed themselves when it became apparent that the pirates had won the battle. The women suspected that torture lay ahead.

The Great Mogul was furious upon learning of the brutal treatment of those aboard the *Gang-i-Sawai* and stopped all trade with England until the Crown appropriately dealt with Avery. Just like Captain Kidd, Avery was unaware he was a wanted man. When Avery arrived in the Bahamas and learned of his predicament, he tried to bribe Governor Trott with one thousand pounds of elephant tusks. The buccaneer also sold the *Fancy* to the governor at a cheap price. The governor then informed the pirate that although he had allowed him to stay at New Providence, he didn't have the authority to pardon him. Meanwhile, the English government, anxious to appease the Mogul, offered a £500 reward for Avery. The East India Company, also hoping to pacify India, offered a £1,000 reward for him. Although in the past the East India Company had subtly encouraged piracy in its trade wars, it had to take the side of justice in regard to Henry Avery–India was threatening the lives of English colonists until justice was done.

The pirate crew dissolved at this point. Some went to America to spend their fortune; others went to England and Ireland where they were eventually arrested. Altogether, twenty-four pirates were captured and six hanged. However, the shrewd pirate captain was not one of the men appre-

The treasure included many items, but most noteworthy were the dozens and dozens of diamonds, solid-gold plates, a jewel-studded saddle handmade for the Mogul himself, and bags of gold and silver coins.

hended. Just what happened to Henry Avery?

The sea robber certainly was able to retire from piracy after his colossal haul. It is believed he first went to America to trade with the poor states that welcomed buccaneers, such as New York, Massachusetts, and North Carolina. There were reported sightings of him from cafés in Paris to far-flung corners of the world.

The only thing we know with certainty is that Avery ended up in England when his money ran out. He had taken most of his cut of the loot in diamonds. In order to convert the gems to cash, he had to rely on diamond merchants–the kind of dealers who would be very discreet. Old friends of his, whom he deemed trustworthy, took the gems to the diamond merchants since it wasn't safe for him to go to Bristol.

Avery stayed in Biddiford and waited for his friends to return with his money. They never came back. Finally, out of desperation, Avery journeyed to Bristol where he discovered that his "friends" and the diamond merchants had tricked the reformed pirate out of his precious stones, leaving him with nothing. Not long thereafter, Avery fell ill and died on the tenth of June in the first year of the reign of King George III. The pauper was buried in a churchyard in Biddiford by its parish.

• • • • •

More about Henry Avery

Ironically, William Kidd, who later became famous for his

attack on India's *Quedagh Merchant*, was given a privateering commission because England wanted to prevent attacks on Indian ships, such as the brutal assault on the Mogul's ship by Henry Avery. The commission permitted the capture of pirates who might attack Indian ships.

. . . . .

The play, *Successful Pyrate*, was based on the exploits of Henry Avery.

. . . . .

One interesting and highly disputed tale has it that Avery made the Mogul's daughter, who was aboard the *Gang-i-Sawai*, his lover. He reportedly took her to Madagascar where she died of a broken heart after their baby was stillborn.

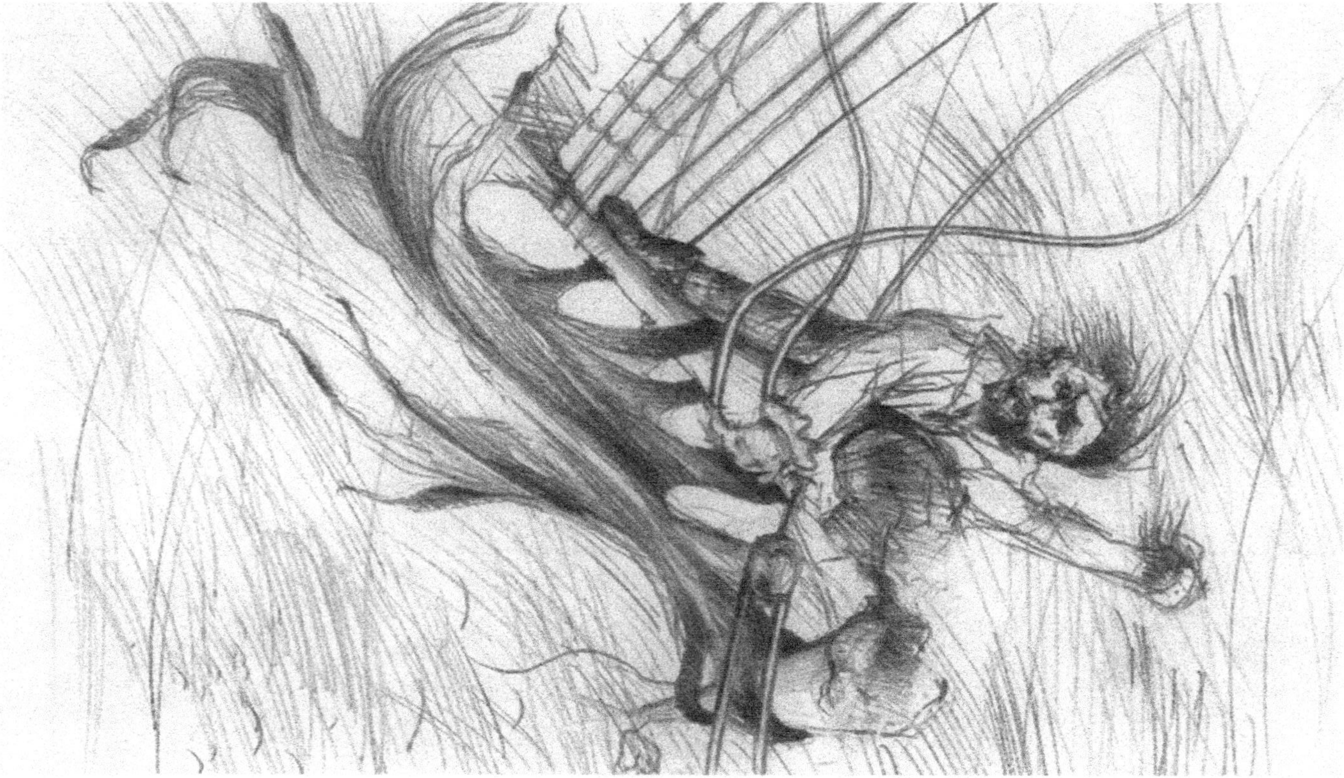

Julie Rabun

William "Billy" Lewis

His crew believed William Lewis was a disciple of the Devil.

By the time he was eleven, Lewis was sailing with pirate Captain Banister. He had met the buccaneer while hanging around Boston Harbor. Claiming him as his nephew, Banister took the boy to sea with him. This lifestyle suited the lad to a tee until the ship was captured by the British navy and its crew taken to Port Royal, Jamaica for trial. Billy Lewis told the officers that he and a boy he had befriended named Darby McCaffrey had been forced into servitude. As a result of this lie, the boys were freed.

The teens signed on with a merchant ship almost immediately thereafter. For five years the two friends enjoyed an idyllic life of seeing the world and obeying no rules. Then, the vessel was captured by Spanish pirates at Havana. The pirates worked the youths like slaves. Conditions on the ship were terrible, and food was scarce. Lewis, McCaffrey, and six others escaped in a canoe. In time, they captured a Spanish boat, and some of the men joined forces with them. The pirates continued to overtake fishing boats until they had enough men to be a real crew. Billy Lewis was the appointed leader of approximately forty men, and his longtime friend, Darby McCaffrey, served as his quartermaster.

The pirates learned from a captured schooner that there was a big prize nearby. A sleek ten-gun sloop was bound from Jamaica to the Bay of Campeachy. Lewis sent a note to the sloop, "Sell your ship for 10,000 pieces-of-eight or face the consequences."

When Captain Tucker read this note, he knew he was in big trouble. He tried to gather men from nearby ships to help stop the buccaneer. Tucker warned the other ships that his sloop was only the first of the intended victims. They would all be captured eventually if they didn't band together now.

However, the other captains didn't want to fight. Instead, they planned to escape in their smaller, faster vessels if it looked like the pirate was going to attack. Ironically, Captain Tucker escaped while Lewis successfully assaulted the ten Bermuda sloops whose captains had refused to help Tucker.

One vessel could have gotten away, but when Lewis fired a shot in its direction, the captain immediately surrendered. He also disclosed the cargo to the pirate captain before he asked! The freebooter was so furious at the captain's cowardly attitude and unprovoked betrayal of the ship's owner that he beat the man fiercely.

Then, Lewis picked the biggest and best ship of the bunch, a 90-ton sloop, and claimed it. He armed it with twelve cannons and renamed it the *Morning Star*. The captain now had a crew of eighty men. They took prizes all along the southeastern seaboard, particularly Florida and South Carolina. At Charleston, many of the men who were reluctant pirates abandoned their leader.

Like most sea robbers who found their way to this port town, Captain Lewis liked the place. He lingered in Charleston, cleaning his vessel and trading with local merchants, who were especially grateful for his rum and sugar. The pirates also stole rum, sugar, spices, meats, fabrics, and coins from merchant ships. Lewis learned that his English pirates planned to take over the ship and maroon the French crew members and himself. To thwart this scheme, Lewis and his men triumphantly attacked the dissenting pirates. As a result, all English crew members were put into a boat, given a small ration of beef, and set adrift. Captain Lewis left South Carolina and headed for Virginia, where he stayed and plundered for a while before he returned to South Carolina. Next, the sea robber sailed to Newfoundland and Conception Bay. While there he took one of New Providence Governor Woodes Rogers' vessels, the *Herman*, a twenty-four-gun galley. The ship's master, Captain Beal, told the buccaneer to send his quartermaster and Beal would load him up with supplies if Lewis didn't initiate any more attacks. Incredibly, the pirate captain fell for this trick and sent Darby McCaffrey ashore.

The quartermaster was captured and taken to Woodes Rogers. Despite Lewis's best efforts, he could not free his friend. Determined not to leave McCaffrey behind, Lewis switched tactics. He attacked a couple of ships and took all aboard as prisoners. One captive was Captain Beal's brother. He sent word to Rogers he would kill him if McCaffrey was not returned. The quartermaster was quickly freed!

After McCaffrey was safely on the pirate ship and had assured Lewis he had been well treated, Lewis released the hostages. Later, McCaffrey revealed that he had been chained to a sheet anchor. When Lewis angrily demanded to know why McCaffrey hadn't told him of this before he let the prisoners go, his friend replied he hadn't wanted to see innocent people hurt for the actions of others.

Unbeknownst to Captain Lewis, the bleakest time of his life was about to begin when he determined to take a twenty-four cannon French ship. The sea villains were no match for the heavily armed vessel and its watchful captain, so Lewis waited until some of the French crew left in fishing boats and then seized them. He then replaced the crew in the two boats with his own men. No one aboard the French vessel paid attention to the boats as they approached because they thought it was their own men returning from a fishing expedition. The pirates were able to launch a conquering assault. Not only did Lewis switch ships with the French captain, but many of the French crew eagerly signed on with the pirate. Lewis now had a crew of over two hundred men, as well as a flotilla. But, the prize had come at a great cost. His long-time friend, Darby McCaffrey, had been killed during the confrontation.

After the death of his friend, the sea villain headed for Guinea and began to act bizarrely. With reckless abandon, he took ships of many origins–Portuguese, Dutch, and English. He became withdrawn, choosing to keep to himself most of the time. The pirate even took to talking to himself. Speculation began that Lewis was carrying on conversations with the Devil.

Not long after this, he was in pursuit of a prize off the waters of South Carolina when he lost part of his masts.

Lewis climbed up to the remnants of the topmast. Upon reaching the pinnacle, he yanked out a clump of his hair and held it up to the sky. "Good Devil, take this until I come!" he screamed at the top of his lungs. Strangely, Lewis's ship did pick up speed and soon overtook the other ship, allowing for a successful raid.

His men started to believe Lewis had a bond with the Devil, and that really frightened them—so much so that many talked of getting rid of Lewis. Some of his loyal men tried to warn him, but their words fell on deaf ears. Lewis muttered only one sentence in response to these men's admonition. Some accounts claim Lewis said, "When the Devil comes to claim my soul, there is nothing anyone can do to prevent it." Other accounts state he said, "I cannot withstand my destiny. The Devil told me I will be murdered tonight." That night, some of the French crew came into his cabin and murdered Captain William Lewis while he was asleep.

· · · · ·

More about "Billy" Lewis

It is unclear whether Lewis was French or English. Regardless, he had an aptitude for language and spoke French, Spanish, and English, as well as some obscure languages, including that of the Mosquil Indians.

Stede Bonnet
Gentleman Pirate

Bonnet's story is incredibly appealing because most men take up piracy to get rich. However, Bonnet was already well-to-do. Why he took up piracy can only be surmised.

Stede Bonnet led a disciplined life as an officer in the Colonial Militia. After his service, Bonnet took up residence at his family's sugar plantation in the British colony of Barbados and became a successful planter. Without warning, the well-respected gentleman bought a ship and took up piracy! It was a titanic shock to everyone who knew him. Most believed he must have lost his mind,

Bonnet holds a distinct place in pirate history. He is reportedly the only pirate who bought his own ship. Even William Kidd had backers who helped pay for the *Adventure Galley*. Also, while William Kidd continually claimed to be a privateer, Stede Bonnet never denied he was a pirate.

presuming he suffered from dementia brought on by his miserable marriage.

While it was true that there was no love lost between him and his nagging wife, the shrew was probably not the real reason Bonnet sought such a dramatically different career. More likely, he, like William Kidd, was terribly bored with his new lifestyle. Barbados may have been beautiful, but it didn't offer much excitement. He was accustomed to the action and melodrama of the military, and now each day was the same as the day before.

•　•　•　•　•

Bonnet named his vessel the *Revenge* and equipped it with ten guns and a crew of seventy, including experienced quartermaster Israel Morton. Soon after his voyage began, Captain Bonnet successfully assaulted the *Turbet* (Barbados), the *Endeavour* and the *Young* (Scotland), and the *Anne* (Virginia). Bonnet burned every Barbadian vessel he captured to keep news of his escapades and whereabouts secret. Things were going well until he reached the waters of the Carolinas.

By then his crew, who had been hired by Quartermaster Morton, had determined that they didn't have a strong leader. The men had nothing in common with Bonnet and couldn't relate to him. Bonnet wasn't much of a drinker, and by anyone's standards, the man dressed outrageously. He was no sea dog, either–as a matter of fact, he suffered from seasickness.

It was there in the Carolina waters that the buccaneer met up with Blackbeard. It was Bonnet's saving grace that the fierce pirate captain was amused by the dapper gentleman.

Stede Bonnet loved to dress extravagantly. He could be seen wearing ensembles featuring dark trousers and a white shirt with ruffled front and oversized sleeves, as well as colorful vests.

•　•　•　•　•

Blackbeard also liked Bonnet's sloop. He basically took over the *Revenge*, adding it to his growing flotilla, but he allowed Bonnet to continue to sail with him. At first their association was under the guise of being more or less partners. Soon, however, Blackbeard made one of his own men commander of the *Revenge* but kept Bonnet aboard. This arrangement seemed to sit well with Bonnet. He knew the ships were unlikely to be attacked with Blackbeard as their leader, and there would be no question of mutiny while the legendary "Fury from Hell" was in charge.

For three months in early 1718, the whereabouts of Blackbeard, Bonnet, and their crew are unknown. Soon after they resurfaced, Blackbeard pulled his famous Blockade of Charleston (known as Charles Town at that time). After this, the "Black-faced Devil" knew he had to cut Bonnet loose. Now that Blackbeard was plundering Colonial America and not the open seas, he had more ships and crew than he needed. Dividing up the booty so many ways was no longer acceptable.

The corsair told Bonnet and his men that work needed to be done on the *Queen Anne's Revenge*. He also said it was best for all of them to hide out until they received pardons for their dastardly assault on Charleston. Blackbeard took the ships into Beaufort Inlet (formerly known as Topsail Inlet), then sent Bonnet and some of his men ashore to check on the pardons and obtain some provisions. Bonnet was reluctant to go, probably sensing trouble, but in the end did leave.

Immediately after Bonnet's departure, Blackbeard, the ruthless pirate commander, had Bonnet's remaining men transport anything of value on the *Revenge* to a smaller ship. After that, Blackbeard and his ships took off for Bath, England, pausing just long enough to maroon some of Bonnet's men on a sandbar.

When Bonnet returned, he discovered what Blackbeard had done. He rescued the marooned men and set out in search of Blackbeard to get revenge. It was to his advantage that he didn't find the ruthless freebooter since Bonnet was no match for Blackbeard.

During this time, Bonnet changed his name to Captain Thomas since his pardon was in the name of Stede Bonnet. In keeping with his new identity, he also changed the name of his ship from *Revenge* to *Royal James*. As Captain Thomas, the pirate captured many great prizes around Delaware Bay and Virginia.

Before he could continue sailing, however, he had to do some work on the *Royal James*, including recaulking. This work was done at a cove near the mouth of the Cape Fear River. Word of his location came to the attention of South Carolina Governor Johnson. The governor sent Colonel William Rhett to nab the pirate captain. Colonel Rhett led two eight-gun sloops, the *Henry* and the *Sea Nymph*, with a combined crew of 130 men. It is unclear whether Rhett was really sent to capture Bonnet or the governor believed that the notorious pirate Captain Charles Vane was hiding there and Rhett found Bonnet while seeking Vane.

When Bonnet saw Colonel Rhett's ships coming his way,

he knew he was not prepared for such an attack and tried to flee. Unfortunately, his ship ran aground on a sandbar, but so did Rhett's ships. For hours, gunfire was exchanged. Finally after five or six hours of battle, Bonnet surrendered and the pirates were brought to Charleston. It was not until this point that Rhett discovered Captain Thomas and Stede Bonnet were one and the same!

Many believed Bonnet would be shown mercy and clemency at his trial, but he was not so confident. Bonnet felt sure he would be served up as an example and could already feel the noose around his neck. So Bonnet and his sailing master, David Herriot, escaped (either by trickery or bribery). It wasn't very difficult since Bonnet was barely guarded. Coming from an aristocratic background, he was treated better than other captured pirates. After all, he was nicknamed the "Gentleman Pirate," and it was thought he could be expected to behave as such. Obviously not!

Even if leniency would have been shown to the pirate before the escape attempt, there would be no mercy for the once-pardoned sea villain afterwards. Governor Johnson offered a £700 reward for the capture of Stede Bonnet and his sidekick, Herriot–dead or alive. Meanwhile, the pair stole a boat, but Colonel Rhett caught up with them and Herriot was killed during this recapture effort. Bonnet was apprehended and taken back to Charleston in October 1718. Not only did Justice Trott sentence Bonnet and his men to death by public hanging, he also subjected them to an extraordinarily lengthy speech.

Here are some excerpts of that speech:

> You know that the Crimes you have committed are *evil* in themselves, and contrary to the *Light* and *Law* of *Nature*, as well as the *Law* of God, by which you are commanded that *you shall* not *steal,*

Exodus 20.15. And the Apostle St. Paul express affirms, That *Thieves shall not inherit the Kingdom of God*, 1 Cor. 6.10.

You being a Gentleman that have had the Advantage of a *liberal Education*, and being generally esteemed a *Man of Letters*, I believe it will be needless for me to explain to you the Nature of *Repentance* and *Faith* in Christ, they being so fully and so often mentioned in the Scriptures, that you cannot but know them. And therefore, perhaps, for that Reason it might be thought by some improper for me to have said so much to you, but that considering the Course of your Life & Actions, I have just Reason to fear, that the Principles of Religion that had been instilled into you by your *Education*, have been at least corrupted, if not entirely defaced, by the *Scepticism* and *Infidelity* of this wicked Age; and that what Time you allow'd for Study, was rather apply'd to the *Polite Literature* & the vain Philosophy of the Times, than a serious Search after the *Law & Will* of God, as revealed unto us in the Holy *Scriptures*: For *had your Delight been in the Law of the Lord, & that you had meditated therein Day and Night*, Psalms 1.2. you would then have found that God's Word was a *Lamp unto your Feet, & a Light to your Path*, Psal. 119.105, and that you would account all other Knowledge but *Loss*, in Comparison of the *Excellency of the Knowledge of Christ Jesus*, Philistines 3.8. *who to them that are called is the Power of God, and the Wisdom of God*, 1 Cor. 1.24. *even the hidden Wisdom which God ordained before the World*, Chapters 2.7.

That you, the said Stede Bonnet, *shall go from hence to*

the Place from whence you came & from thence to the Place of Execution, where you shall be hang'd by the Neck till you are dead.

And the God of infinite Mercy be merciful to your Soul.

On November 8, 1718 all but three of Bonnet's men were hanged. Stede Bonnet's trial started immediately after this, and at the end of it, the "Gentleman Pirate" was hanged at White Point in Charleston, South Carolina. He never disclosed his reason for becoming a pirate.

Thomas Tew

Like William Kidd, he claimed to be a privateer, not a pirate.

Thomas Tew holds a distinctive place in pirate history as one of the few American sea villains who came from a distinguished background. He hailed from Newport, Rhode Island, and his family was very well-to-do. However, Thomas Tew never followed in the conservative steps of his ancestors.

His career as a pirate started when area merchants and businessmen approached Tew to lead their top-secret mission. They needed a competent and trustworthy seaman to fulfill their goal. As a result, they made a generous and private arrangement with him in 1692. Happy with the large percentage he would receive, along with the ship and provisions provided, Tew agreed to lead the mission under one special condition–he made his sponsors get a privateering commission from Bermuda Governor Isaac Richier, which authorized him to attack French ships legally.

For months he got ready for the voyage. The privateer made sure his vessel, *Amity*, was properly stocked and that he had sufficient ammunition for her eight cannons. He selected sixty men whom he knew and trusted as very able seamen. He told them the assignment was to take a French factory, Goree, on the African coast.

In December 1692, Tew and his crew set sail. In truth, Tew probably never intended to carry out his original assignment. Once at sea, he gathered his men and convinced them they could easily capture vessels belonging to the Great Mogul because the ships were large, slow, and poorly equipped for retaliation. He also described the grand riches that were ripe for the taking if they engaged in such piracy. Tew also pointed out there would be no reward for destroying the French factory. That mission only profited a handful of men, he explained. Was it worth their bravery? Was it worth risking their lives?

The crew didn't need much persuading since the men's pay was based solely on their cut of any plunder obtained, and they had strong confidence in their leader. "A gold chain or a wooden leg, we'll stand by you!" they chorused. Ready to be rich beyond their wildest dreams, they turned the *Amity* towards the Cape of Good Hope and then the Red Sea. Much like Captain Kidd, Tew had trouble fulfilling his promise. Weeks went by with no prospects. Thousands and thousands of miles later, the men still had nothing to show for their dedication. But, unlike Kidd's crew, Tew's men never questioned ultimate success. They stuck by their leader,

About Pirate Crews

Pirate *captains* were typically elected. The men chose the leader based on how tough and terrifying he was. He was also expected to be a very good navigator.

The *quartermaster*, who was second in command, was the only other elected officer. He was also in charge of dividing and distributing booty, assigning punishment, and overseeing prisoners. During a voyage he was considered more powerful than the captain, who was primarily in charge during battle. The quartermaster was the voice of the crew.

A *boatswain* was in charge of rigging, sails, and ship maintenance. He had a special whistle which he used to issue commands to other crew members in regard to rigging and sails.

A *gunner* was in charge of the ship's armament and crew members who handled arms.

A *sailing master* was in charge of navigation.

Other noteworthy members include the first mate, surgeon, carpenter, musicians, and sailmakers.

believing their patience would be greatly rewarded. The question of whether the crew's faith and perseverance was worthwhile was answered when Tew spied a Mogul ship in the distance through his looking glass, and gave orders to give chase. As the pirates overtook it and began their assault, they received an ugly surprise.

Between three and five hundred Indian soldiers were on board, ready to defend the Great Mogul's cargo. Astounded, Tew's men abruptly ceased their aggression. But when their leader continued the assault, shouting about the great wealth they nearly had, his men quickly came to his aid and were soon crying "Victory!"

Astonishingly, not one pirate was critically injured or killed during the confrontation! Additionally, their courage was rewarded with £100,000 in gold and silver, as well as ivory, silk, and exotic spices. The men carried the spoils onto the *Amity* and sailed off. Fueled by their success, Captain Tew was ready to continue, but the quartermaster refused.

•   •   •   •   •

They proceeded to a favorite pirate hideout, St. Mary's Island (now called Sainte-Marie), near Madagascar. Here, they divvied up the treasure and secured the sponsors' share in the hold. The men's loyalty was duly rewarded. Every member of the crew received £3,000 (equivalent to around $3.5 million today) and they proceeded to celebrate their new wealth. Twenty to twenty-five of his men, pleased by the climate and treatment the native women gave them, decided they wouldn't return with Tew.

The men also spent time cleaning and repairing the sloop for the long trip home. While this work was being done, the buccaneer met up with another famous freebooter, Captain Mission, who invited Tew to spend time with him at a pirate colony he had established called Libertatia. Intrigued,

Tew agreed, and during this time, the men became good friends. Thomas Tew was made admiral of the growing colony. He recommended building an arsenal and expanding the naval force. The other "officials" agreed to the arsenal but did not see the necessity of more naval power.

There has been and still is great debate by historians as to whether this colony, referred to as Libertatia, ever existed.

.   .   .   .   .

Next, Tew set sail on the *Victoire*, hoping to encounter East India trade ships from which to gain volunteers to join this new "nation." Tew firmly believed that Libertatia needed a much bigger population in order to gain strength and recognition. While he was carrying out his twofold mission, the colony was savagely attacked by a native tribe. During this assault, most of the pirate inhabitants, including many of Tew's men, were killed.

Like Tew, Mission was away during the attack, and when the two men met later, Tew tried to convince his friend to come to America with him. Mission refused. He told his fellow pirate he might go to Europe. The pair decided to sail together for as much of their journey as possible. During this time, they ran into a bad storm and both men fought to keep their vessels afloat. Mission's ship was lost along with the lives of those aboard, but Tew managed to save both his ship and men.

After a year at sea and months en route home, Captain Tew arrived at Newport harbor, Rhode Island, in April 1694. He had attempted to reach Bermuda, but storms prevented it, so he had sailed on to Newport and then sent the promised riches to his sponsors in Bermuda.

Tew's first cruise became known as "the Pirate Round." The route started in North America, crossed the Atlantic Ocean, rounded the tip of Africa on the way to Madagascar, and then headed back. This was a distance of roughly 24,000 miles. After hearing of his prosperity, every sea-roving man from sailors to pirates set out on "the Pirate Round" in hopes of meeting with the same success Thomas Tew had.

The seamen were welcomed like conquering heroes. The success they had achieved was stupendous. The local economy flourished with the influx of trade. Governor Fletcher became a good friend of Tew's, reveling in his stories of life at sea. The governor never tired of hearing how Tew had outfought hundreds of Indian soldiers to obtain the booty. With his wealth, the sea robber established his own shipping fleet, with vessels in North Carolina, New York, Pennsylvania, and Rhode Island.

Tew was doggedly pursued by merchants and government officials to lead another expedition. His crew had exhausted their money and was also anxious for Tew to come out of "retirement." Finally a deal was put on the table he couldn't refuse. Again he was issued a privateering commission, and just seven short months after his return, he departed on another voyage around the world.

•　•　•　•　•

In September 1695, Captain Tew came upon an Indian ship in the Red Sea. Unfortunately for him, the Great Mogul had armed his soldiers better than on previous voyages, and the battle was worse than Tew expected. The air was filled with smoke from the many cannon shots and gunfire. Tew emerged from this hazy scene staggering and clutching his stomach. When the pirate captain took his arms from his abdomen, blood and intestines spilled out of an enormous hole in his stomach. He died within seconds of receiving the wound. Ironically, Tew had secured enough wealth during his first mission to never have to go to sea again—he had barely had a chance to enjoy his money before he was killed.

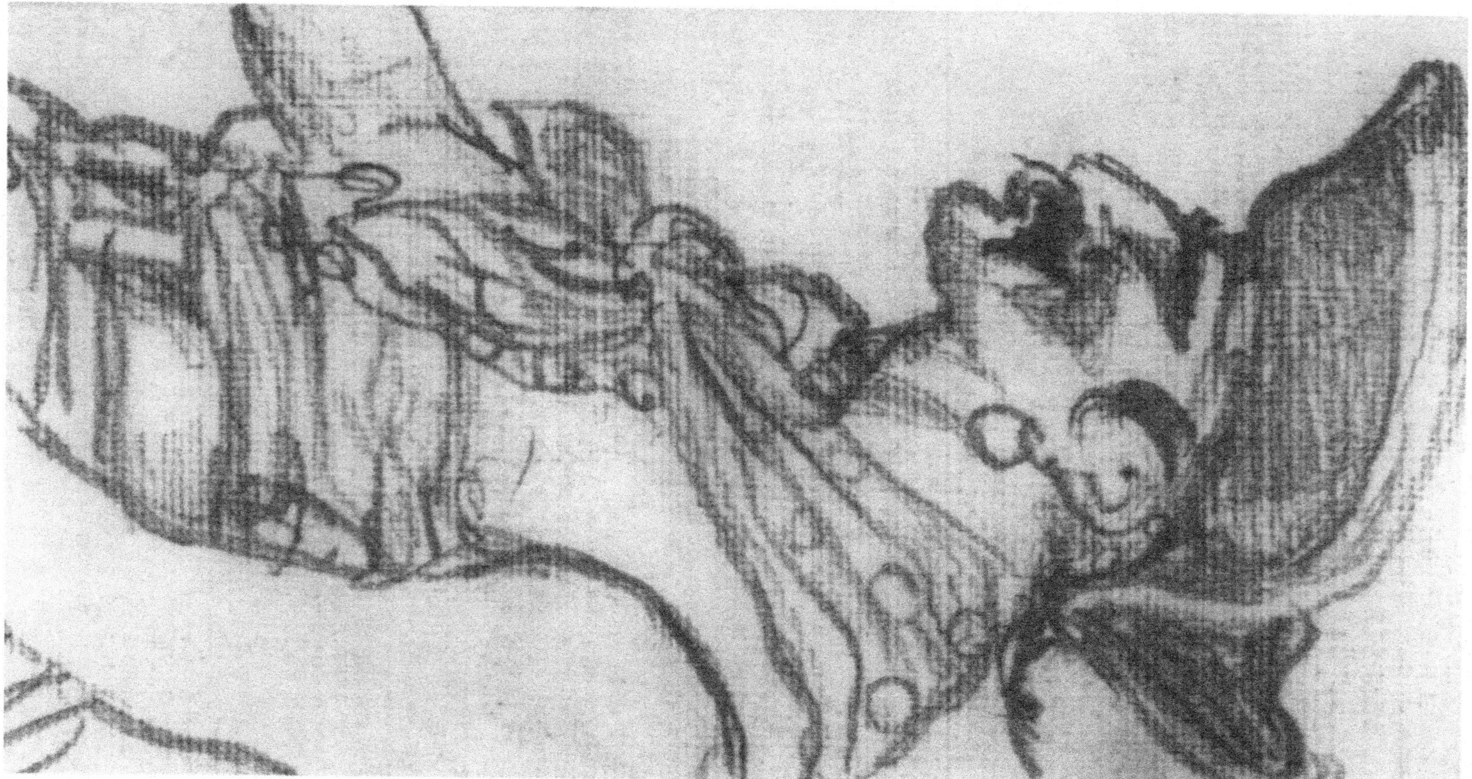

Library of Congress

Richard Worley

Richard Worley began his life of piracy with one tiny boat, a keg of water, and a little food.

Richard Worley became a pirate in September 1718. He, along with eight companions, set sail from New York to the Delaware River in a small boat with only a few old muskets, ammunition, biscuits, a keg of water, and a couple of dried tongues of beef. Before long, the men seized food and other provisions. Next, they met up with a sloop and talked its crew into joining forces with them. At this point the pirates abandoned their open boat and aggressively overtook a few other sloops. In a short time, Worley had gone from one tiny boat and eight men to a sloop equipped with six cannons, several small guns and pistols, and a crew of twenty-five.

At that point, Captain Worley raised the pirate flag to let others know his mission. Soon thereafter, the buccaneers ended up in North Carolina, where they narrowly missed being captured. The ship needed cleaning, so they chose an inlet where the pirates figured they would be hidden until they were finished working on the ship.

However, as part of his campaign to end piracy, South Carolina Governor Johnson had sent men to capture pirates, and these men had learned the whereabouts of the buccaneers. Worley and his men left just minutes before the governor's two ships arrived. Johnson's pirate hunters pursued Worley to the capes of Virginia.

The ships flanked Worley's vessel, from the quarter and bow, and the governor's men swiftly boarded. The buccaneers knew it was hopeless, but they stuck to their agreement to "fight and conquer or die." All the pirates were killed during battle, except Captain Worley and another pirate. The critically wounded men were quickly brought to shore so they could be hanged before they died of their wounds. Worley had been a pirate for only six months when he was hanged in February 1719.

Charles Vane

Charles Vane went into the "pirate hall of fame" when he outsmarted numerous other pirate captains to achieve the mammoth treasure of a sunken Spanish galleon.

A Spanish galleon filled with treasure ran into a reef and sank near Florida. It is reported that hordes of pirates pounced on the half-sunk wreck trying to get at its treasure. Another Spanish ship was sent to collect the fortune, but the crew's efforts were hampered by a band of pirates who were after the same thing. Soon, two Spanish warships arrived and chased away the pirates. After the

Woodes Rogers (disfigured while priva- teering when a musket ball shat- tered his jaw) was best known for his rescue of Alexander Selkirk, a man who had been marooned off the coast of Chile. The story was made famous when Daniel Defoe wrote *Robinson Crusoe*. If anyone could clean up piracy in the Bahamas, England was confident it would be the tough and worldly Woodes Rogers. However, when the former adventurer arrived in the Bahamas, even he silently questioned his ability to accomplish this monumental task.

treasure had safely been loaded onto the Spanish vessel, the warships departed to tend to an urgent problem elsewhere. Pirate Captain Charles Vane had watched his brethren try to get the treasure, but he had patiently waited for a moment such as this. He victoriously raided the ship and retrieved its booty.

Unfortunately for Vane, New Providence (Bahamas) Governor Woodes Rogers had been commissioned to end piracy. He was chosen because he was one of England's biggest and most prosperous adventurers. Rogers was considered a privateer, a businessman, and a terrific sea captain, since he had circumnav- igated the globe.

• • • • •

Rogers offered pirate captains and their crews pardons, despite previous evil deeds. With support from the King, he set out to make examples of those who didn't accept a pardon and go straight. The message was simple: Buccaneers were no longer welcome at this former pirate haven. Trapped at New Providence with his booty, Vane offered to accept the pardon Rogers extended to all the pirates, if Vane could keep his plunder.

To His Excellency The Governor of New Providence

Your Excellency may please to understand that we are willing to accept His Majesty's most gracious pardon on the following terms, viz. That you will suffer us to dispose of all our goods now in our possession. Likewise, to act as we see fit with everything belonging to us, as His Majesty's Act of Grace specifies. If Your Excellency shall please to comply with this we shall with all readiness accept of His Majesty's Act of Grace. If not, we are obliged to stand on our defense.

So conclude
Your humble servants

Charles Vane and company

While Woodes Rogers may have succeeded in ridding the Bahamas of Charles Vane, the pirate captain was considered triumphant since he was the only sea robber to have openly and successfully challenged Governor Rogers.

The letter infuriated Woodes Rogers. There was no way he could extend a pardon for piracy and let pirates keep their loot. What kind of message would that send? The new governor knew he would have to establish his reputation by quickly defeating the arrogant and crafty Charles Vane. As Vane attempted a getaway, Rogers tried to block his ship. But

> **One of Vane's greatest char–acteristics was patience, which served him well as a sea villain. It also separated him from most other pirates. Buccaneers had short fuses and even shorter attention spans. However, Charles Vane's gift of patience usually got him what he wanted.**

the brilliant buccaneer foiled his efforts by setting a ship on fire and pointing it in the direction of Roger's vessel. The men were so busy trying to maneuver their massive ship out of harm's way that they were unable to stop Captain Vane as he, his men, and their treasure blissfully sailed away!

. . . . .

When Rogers drove Vane out of Nassau harbor it became apparent to most pirates that this was a new Bahamas and piracy was not going to be tolerated. Most followed Vane's lead and headed to North Carolina and Virginia. Vane had managed to escape Governor Rogers with a sloop owned by a man named Yeates, and ninety men. En route to Colonial America, he captured a Barbadian ship and made Yeates commander of it.

Next, Vane headed for Hispaniola where he captured a Spanish ship bound for Havana. Next, he successfully assaulted a vessel off St. Christopher. He took the booty from these hauls back to pirate-friendly North Carolina. Now the state endured Blackbeard, Bonnet, and Vane. The pirates took whatever they wanted. Merchant ships entering or departing the port of Charleston were hardest hit. By this time, Vane had supplied well over a hundred men for Yeates. But Vane was still running the show.

Yeates had no real power and was fed up with the situa-tion. In retaliation, he took his ship and crew and escaped into the Edisto River. Vane followed, but when Yeates shot at the approaching vessel, Vane decided it would be better to catch the mutinous pirate by surprise. While searching for an inlet where he could hide and wait, Vane came upon Blackbeard. After this, Vane and his men joined Blackbeard and some other pirates for a party at Ocracoke, North Carolina. This event became known as the "Ocracoke Orgy."

•　　•　　•　　•　　•

Meanwhile, Yeates and his men surrendered in exchange for a pardon. Yeates had ninety slaves aboard his vessel, and he used them as a bargaining chip to help obtain the pardons. The slaves were returned to their owner and subsequently auctioned. As part of the negotiation to be pardoned, Yeates also revealed that the notorious Charles Vane was in the area. South Carolina Governor Johnson sent Colonel William Rhett to capture him.

The savvy pirate captain was gone by the time Rhett's sloops arrived. Near Delaware, Vane encountered a warship. His men pushed him to attack, but Vane sensibly declined. He knew they wouldn't win the battle against a well-armed military crew and vessel. His first mate, John "Calico Jack" Rackham insisted that they could have claimed the warship.

Many of the men began echoing the sentiments of Rackham. A vote was taken. Should Charles Vane remain their captain or should his first mate take over as leader? The crew elected Rackham as captain. Near northwest Jamaica, the new captain put Vane and some of his loyal men on one of their schooners and allowed them to sail away.

This wasn't the end for Vane. In fact, it wasn't long before the resilient buccaneer was back in the game. First, he acquired some guns. Then he was able to take a few substantial prizes, which afforded him a couple of good-sized ships, crew, and loot. At the Bay of Honduras, Vane's ships were

Dories were little more than canoes. They certainly were not sufficient for the open sea.

thrown onto some rocks during a wicked storm. Many of the men were killed instantly. Others were drowned when they were knocked overboard into the sweeping surf. Miraculously, the only one to survive was the "teflon pirate," Charles Vane. He made it to a deserted island. For some time, the only humans to see Vane were sea turtle hunters in dories.

• • • • •

The turtle hunters gave Vane fresh water, and the pirate survived on fish and bananas until a merchant ship anchored at the island. Coincidentally, the ship's leader, Captain Holford, was an old mate of Vane's. Holford had been a pirate, but upon receiving a pardon he had gone legitimate. The merchant captain would not take the pirate aboard, knowing Vane would take over his ship.

"I shan't trust you aboard my ship unless I carry you a Prisoner; for I shall have you caballing with my Men, knock me on the Head, & run away with my Ship a pyrating."

Despite Vane's assurances he would do no such thing, Holford knew a pirate's word meant nothing. He did promise to return in a month's time and take him, as a prisoner, to Port Royal, Jamaica, if he desired. Reportedly, Holford also told Vane he could steal a dory or die, if he was squeamish at the notion of returning to Jamaica.

Another merchant captain stopped at the island soon after Holford's departure. Vane pretended to be a shipwrecked sailor and was taken aboard as a new crew member. Ironically, the ship met up with Captain Holford's. This captain was also a friend of Holford's and invited him on board.

What bad luck for Vane! He was spotted by Holford, who informed the captain of his new hand's real identity. Holford then took Vane prisoner, and within a few days turned him in at Port Royal. This time, Charles Vane did not overcome the odds. He was tried on March 22, 1720. Vane pleaded not guilty, but the court had witnesses, including some of the masters of vessels Vane had "claimed."

At the end of the trial the verdict was read: "That he, the said Charles Vane was guilty of the Piracy, Felony, and Robery charged against him." The pirate was hanged on March 29, along with two other pirates, at Gallows Point, Port Royal, Jamaica.

William Kidd

Pirate or Privateer?

Captain Kidd's life is one of the most fascinating and controversial pirate stories ever told.

Probably the only time William Kidd ever saw the shores of Carolina was when he dropped off John Redfield and hid his treasure on his way to answer charges of piracy. This is assuming the story of Redfield and the legendary treasure is true. We will assume it is and include here the story of one of the most controversial figures in the history of piracy.

115

Kidd was born in Greenock, Scotland, (circa 1645), the son of a poor minister. As soon as he was old enough, he went to sea. The lad served on a pirate ship, *Blessed William*, which later surrendered to the Royal Navy in the Caribbean.

Kidd, who later received a king's pardon, was commissioned as a privateer in King William's War in the West Indies. He served as a brave, competent, and aggressive disciple of the Crown during his privateering days.

He secured his wealth during his twenties and thirties as a result of this privateering, which was mixed with some buccaneering. During this profitable duty, Captain Kidd ended up in New York, which he liked so much that he ultimately made it his home. When his commission was over, the privateer became a successful sea captain and merchant and bought a home on New York's posh Pearl Street. In 1688, William Kidd met a beautiful woman, Sarah Cox, who was the wife of a New York alderman and merchant until her husband fell out of a boat at Staten Island and died. Soon thereafter, she married John Oort, another New York merchant and sea captain. He died in 1691, and the wealthy widow wed Kidd just eleven days after her second husband was buried. The marriage conveniently furthered Kidd's financial status.

On the surface, Kidd settled nicely into matrimony and the community. The couple had two daughters, Sarah and Elizabeth. The Kidd family became very involved parishioners of Trinity Church, where they had their very own pew. William Kidd even bought a country house (in what is now known as Liberty Square, New York) for his old age.

The Kidds were well liked, respected, and affluent members of the community. However, the sea-rover-turned-family-man was not satisfied with his life. In fact, very much like pirate Anne Bonny, he was downright bored and tired of his restrictive social setting. Much as he tried to make it work, William Kidd had a restless soul and a darker side that struggled with this puritanical lifestyle.

At this vulnerable point he was befriended by entrepreneur Robert Livingston. Livingston was a fellow Scotsman also transplanted to New York. The new friend brought him a business proposition that guaranteed not only to drive away Kidd's ennui, but also to make all involved very rich. The dissatisfied seaman liked the idea more and more as he pondered it.

The agreement between the king, Bellomont, Livingston, and Kidd was not uncommon. Wealthy men endorsed by the Crown often made deals with priva-teers, pirate captains, and other seamen to capture pirates and their loot.

The plan was a get-rich scheme involving Robert Livingston, William Kidd, Lord Bellomont (governor of Barbados at that time), and some other backers. The silent partners included powerful men such as the Earl of Orford, the Earl of Romney, John Somers (Lord Chan-cellor), the Duke of Shrewsbury, and Sir Edmund Harrison.

Yes, yes this could work, the former privateer mused. This was a legal way to return to the excitement of plunder and battle. All that was needed was a privateering commission for William Kidd, on behalf of England, to capture pirates and their treasure. King William III did award such a commission to Kidd, with the agreement that the Crown would receive ten percent of his loot.

· · · · ·

Bellomont and the other backers contributed the bulk of the cost of the venture, while Livingston and Kidd put up the remaining amount. Although Lord Bellomont had a title, he possessed little money. In order to get his share, he had to borrow money but figured it would be well worth the risk since more than half the plunder would go to Bellomont and his influential partners; ten percent would go to the Crown; and the remainder would be divided among Kidd, Livingston, and the crew.

The most important stipulation was, if no booty was obtained, Kidd and Livingston agreed to pay back all the money put up by Bellomont and the other backers. This meant if Kidd could not deliver his end of the bargain, he would be bankrupt and in debt. The crew was on a "no prey, no pay" basis, which meant plunder was their only pay. To agree to such conditions, Kidd must have been extremely confident of his ability to obtain great treasure by challenging some of the most successful pirates alive.

Kidd went to England and received two passes on December 11, 1695; one allowed him to capture pirates and the other, a Commission of Reprisals, gave him the authority to assault and plunder French ships, should he come upon them. His commission empowered him to "apprehend, seize, and take the Ships, Vessels, and Goods belonging to the French King or his Subjects or Inhabitants within the dominions of the said French King; and such other Ships, Vessels, and Goods as are or shall be liable to confiscation." The passes were clear, however, regarding all other vessels he may come across–"...that you do not, in any manner, offend or molest any of our Friends or Allies, their Ships or Subjects."

An advantage Kidd had over the pirates was his ship, the 287-ton, 125-foot *Adventure Galley*, which had been specially built, albeit as cheaply as possible, for this mission. She was fast, equipped with three huge sails totaling 3,200 yards of canvas, thirty-two oars (in case there was no wind), and numerous guns. To work this great vessel, Kidd needed 150 men. He handpicked seventy sailors, but had difficulty finding more men of the caliber he wanted. Since he had to go back to New York to take care of some business, he decided to round up the other eighty men there.

The privateer met with his first setback before ever leaving English waters. His ship passed a Royal Navy vessel en route to the English Channel. Kidd did not dip his colors (flag) as custom required. Instead, some of his crew made an insulting gesture by turning their backs to the navy ship and then repeatedly slapping their rear ends. For their disrespect, and to teach their captain a lesson, the Royal Navy carried off many of Kidd's best men. Captain Kidd was not acknowledged as he protested and flashed his commission papers. The men Kidd ended up with turned out to be hard-core criminals and other undesirables, the very men he had carefully avoided when hiring a crew!

Why hadn't Kidd simply lowered his flag and stopped his men's crude and insulting behavior? One historian believes it was Kidd's ultimate dream to be commander of the Royal Navy, and so he was resentful that he should have to show deference to a Royal Navy ship. It is also thought that Captain Kidd saw himself on equal footing with the Royal Navy. After all, they were both on missions for the Crown. Why should he humble himself if they were all servants to the king? It could also be that William Kidd had never gotten over the time when he was part of a pirate crew that had been caught by the Royal Navy.

More bad news awaited the privateer when he reached New York. It seems no good seamen were interested in his "no prey, no pay" deal. In desperation, Captain Kidd was forced to accept men whose character or capabilities he doubted. What he ended up with were assorted sailors, thugs, vagabonds, pirates, privateers, and gentlemen attracted by excitement and riches who were unprepared for what lay ahead. Although Kidd reached New York around the fourth of July, it was the fifth of September before he departed to fulfill his assignment.

Heading for Madagascar, Malabar, and the Red Sea region, he again encountered the Royal Navy on December 12, 1696 near Capetown, Africa. After showing his commission papers, he was well received. Royal Navy Commodore Warren invited Kidd aboard for drinks. While the men drank, Warren told Kidd that the navy ship was short-handed and asked the privateer for some of his men. Not only did Kidd refuse, but he also informed the commodore that he needed a new mainsail to replace the one destroyed in a storm.

Shocked when Warren rejected his request, Captain Kidd again stated he needed sails for his mission on behalf of the Crown. The commander again refused, growing more and more angry at Kidd's insistence for help. This time the privateer threatened to seize the needed sails from the first merchant ship he saw if assistance wasn't given. This was the final straw for Commodore Warren, who told the belligerent captain he would take thirty of his best men the following morning to supplement the navy's deficit crew. Captain Kidd reluctantly agreed and returned to his vessel.

As he boarded his ship, he paused long enough to eye the mighty oars that lined both sides of his ship's deck, and the seaman nodded approvingly. During the night, the *Adventure Galley* quietly rowed away! Captain Kidd could not afford to lose any more men and had no intention of handing over even one man to the Royal Navy. By the time Warren discovered Kidd's deception, the privateer was long gone. Kidd may

Passes (flags) were used as part of a bluffing game. Privateers and merchants alike tried to trick each other by raising appropriate passes. Privateers would raise the pass of the ship they intended to attack. In this case, Kidd had the right to attack French ships so he raised a French pass, although his was an English ship. The merchant vessels also carried passes other than their own, so when the captain saw Kidd raise the French pass, he produced his French pass. This was done so Kidd would perceive the ship as another French vessel and not a foe, thus preventing an assault.

How was one to know when a pass was legitimate and when it was not? That was the rub! Often, whether passes were legiti-mate or not didn't matter to the English government since privateering/pirating was so profitable. Unfortunately, for William Kidd, this mentality would all change before his commission was over.

have gotten away, but once again he had alienated the Royal Navy.

Finally, captain and crew reached their destination, which was northwest of Madagascar. By this time, it had been discovered that the ship leaked. More important, provisions were running low, and Kidd's men were getting impatient. They started to question their leader's ability to get the promised plunder.

Then a more devastating event overtook them. Plague wiped out fifty men, which was a third of the crew. With no choice, the captain had to recruit crew replacements in Madagascar. He signed up thirty pirates. He then fixed his sails and with brave determination set forth to apprehend sea robbers and French merchant ships.

Days came and went without reward. More days passed and still nothing. No pirates. No French ships. Nothing. No matter where he went, from Madagascar to the Red Sea, the pirates eluded him. Kidd grew increasingly nervous that there might be a mutiny. The bigger picture was even more grim. If the crew didn't take over the ship, he had to report his failure to his backers and face the dire consequences. His judgment, clouded by the increased grumbling of his men and the ticking clock, led him to attack Dutch, Portuguese, and Moorish merchant ships. He took one Moorish ship and kept its captain, an Englishman named Parker, as well as a Portuguese man, Don Antonio. Kidd needed them as pilot and interpreter, respectively. He convinced himself that under the circumstances his backers would protect him from recriminations.

Once he mistakenly assaulted an English merchant vessel. Upon realizing his error, Kidd released the captain and apologized profusely. The crew sullenly watched the freed merchant ship and its cargo sail away.

• • • • •

Captain Kidd's men, particularly a gunner named William Moore, were extremely unhappy with Kidd's insistence that they leave the English vessel alone. Moore challenged his captain in front of the rest of the crew. The two men shouted hostilities at one another until Captain Kidd, in a moment of utter fury, hurled an iron and wooden bucket at William Moore. It hit him squarely in the head and the gunner died the following morning of a fractured skull. "Damn him, he is a villain!" was Kidd's only response to the news.

Soon after this, the captain mistakenly attacked another ship under English command. But this time he was unable to control his motley crew. They weren't about to surrender the first loot they had managed to obtain during their lengthy voyage.

Reports vary greatly as to just how much the treasure was worth. Estimates range from £12,000 to £710,000. Many experts agree it was £710,000. What we do know is that Kidd's treasure consisted of at least sixty pounds of gold; one hundred pounds of silver; and £10,000 worth of fabric, including muslins, brocades, and silks.

From this point on, American, British, and Indian governments considered Kidd to be no better than any other sea villain. He had acquired this bad reputation although none of his aggressions had led to any real plunder. How must Kidd have felt now? It had been eighteen months since he left England, and he had absolutely nothing to show for it. He finally realized that the task he had undertaken was impossible–there were no pirates or French ships to be found. As Kidd was contemplating his imminent failure and bankruptcy, he saw a large vessel on the horizon. It was obvious the ship was a merchant vessel, and by the looks of it, it was

There is reason to believe that Captain Kidd could have captured pirates if he had so desired, but either the crew wouldn't help or Kidd was more concerned with bringing back treasure than buccaneers. Most likely, both things were true. His crew was interested purely in plunder, and Captain Kidd knew that his backers were most interested in riches as well.

carrying substantial cargo. On January 30, 1698, Captain Kidd gave orders, and *Adventure Galley* assaulted the *Quedagh Merchant.*

When he went aboard the vessel, it was apparent it was a ship belonging to the Great Mogul (the Indian Emperor of Delhi), not a French sloop. Dismissing this Indian identity under the category of a technicality, Kidd robbed the ship of its precious cargo. Gold, silver, jewels, silks, armament, and food were swiftly loaded onto Captain Kidd's ship. As this transfer was being accomplished, a man identified himself as Captain John Wright and revealed he was the real master of *Quedagh Merchant.* This man's English nationality meant Kidd had taken a vessel under English command. The buccaneer, however, continued the raid. He knew his men would never give back the considerable treasure, and he himself was not interested in surrendering booty that would answer all his prayers. An Armenian merchant on board tried to ransom the ship, but the pirates kept both his money and the ship.

After the heist, Kidd hid out long enough to prepare for the long journey home. He also tried to capture some pirates they chanced to encounter, but his crew refused when they discovered who the sea robbers were–the nefarious Captain

Culliford and his men. Kidd probably believed that bringing back the captured pirates and the booty would cancel out his questionable actions. Instead, his crew insisted on taking their part of the riches, and after doing so, most abandoned their leader at Madagascar to crew for pirate Captain Culliford.

• • • • •

Meanwhile, unbeknownst to the sea dog, the Indian Mogul halted all trade with England as a result of Kidd's attack and demanded that the Crown take severe action against him. They were especially offended because a high-ranking official of the court of the Great Mogul had been aboard the *Quedagh Merchant*.

By this time it was June of 1698, and Kidd knew he had to get home as quickly as possible in order to attempt to clear his name. Since *Adventure Galley* was no longer seaworthy, he readied the *Quedagh Merchant* for the long voyage, while recruiting what crew he could. As William Kidd sailed home, he was oblivious to the fact that he was considered a criminal and that no amount of talking on his part would redeem him.

It wasn't until the ship reached the Caribbean, that he and his crew discovered they were wanted men. Kidd tried to calm his men by telling them he could obtain protection from the rich and influential men who had backed the venture, including his good friend Lord Bellomont. His reassurances fell on deaf ears. He convinced only a dozen or so of his men to continue with him.

Kidd got rid of the *Quedagh Merchant* and purchased a small, fast sloop named *Antonio*. Meanwhile, the king, hoping to end piracy, offered pardons to all pirates except Kidd and Avery, because they had severely antagonized the Great Mogul.

Just off New York's east end of Long Island
lies Gardiner's Island, at the mouth of
Peconic Bay. The island was deeded to the
Gardiner family by King Charles II of
England, and it is still owned by that family
today. It was a favorite place for pirates
because of its many coves and its proximity
to New York. From a hill on the island,
lookouts could easily see if anyone was
coming by land. If so, the Atlantic Ocean
was right there, allowing an easy escape.
Pirates met "middlemen" on Gardiner's
Island. These were men who were willing to
buy the booty and give the sea robbers
money on the spot. The goods were
unloaded once terms had been agreed
upon. The wholesalers then rowed the
goods over to Long Island, and at that point
took land transport to New York City to
resell the goods to shop keepers.

Reportedly, while on Gardiner's
Island, William Kidd asked Mrs. Gardiner
to roast a pig for him and his crew.
According to Mrs. Gardiner's great, great
granddaughter, the woman was afraid to

refuse. In return, Kidd gave her a "piece of cloth of gold." According to Harold T. Wilkin's book, *Captain Kidd and His Skeleton Island: The Discovery of a Strange Secret Hidden for 266 Years*, this cloth of gold came from the marriage furniture of one of the Great Mogul's daughters, which was aboard the *Quedagh Merchant* when Kidd took the ship.

Another story indicates a diamond was lost on Gardiner's Island while Kidd's treasure was being sorted. It was later found by Mr. Gardiner, who wanted to take it to Governor Bellomont. His wife talked him out of it, convincing him they would get in trouble for hosting Kidd. The diamond remained in the Gardiner family for many generations. It is unknown what eventually happened to the diamond.

While all of Kidd's treasure concealed in New York may have been recovered, that may not be all there was. It is also popularly believed Kidd hid part of his treasure on North Carolina's Money Island, as well as Sullivan's Island, South Carolina.

· · · · ·

With three years and over 40,000 miles behind him, the sea dog reached New York in June 1699. He discovered that during his absence Bellomont had been made governor of New York and Massachusetts Bay. So, he sent a friend of his, a lawyer by the name of James Emmott, to talk to Bellomont on his behalf. Emmott journeyed to Boston to plea Kidd's case, explaining the extenuating circumstances that led Kidd to commit the illegal acts. The lawyer also produced a letter from Kidd, which detailed his "difficulties" and subsequent actions. Emmott also gave Bellomont the two passes granted for attacking ships bearing French colors and for capturing pirates.

Bellomont promised to protect his "friend" but at the same time wrote a letter to England explaining it was a ruse to get William Kidd near enough to arrest. A jubilant and trusting Kidd, along with his family and maid, traveled to Boston. They arrived on July 1 and stayed in the home of another family friend, Duncan Campbell.

Bellomont was hospitable, but insisted on seeing Captain Kidd's shiplog. When Kidd explained it had been destroyed by his crew, the governor gave him instructions to write a detailed account of his journey and promptly give it to him.

When the designated time expired, Kidd still had not finished the journal. He begged for more time and was granted a very small extension. Bellomont told the sea captain to bring what he had written to Bellomont's home that evening. Kidd took this as a good sign and hurried back to his quarters to continue accounting the events of the past three years. That evening, Kidd, clutching his freshly penned journal, made it through the gate and partway up the entry walk to Bellomont's house before he was arrested! Even his wife was jailed briefly, and some of their household possessions were taken, as well as what loot could be found.

Some accounts report that the confiscated possessions were all the sea dog had, while other reports indicate he buried much more in New York and the Carolinas.

. . . . .

Kidd's wife was soon freed, but the rebellious seaman was detained in Boston's Stone Prison. Before long, the discovered spoils of the *Quedagh Merchant* raid, along with William Kidd, were shipped back to England for the king and trial, respectively. Kidd's fate was sealed because of two things. First, Bellomont had gotten greedy. He wanted the sea captain's share of the treasure, in addition to his own. Second, William Kidd was a source of embarrassment to his sponsors, Lord Romney and Admiral Russell among them. They were cast in a very unfavorable light when the secret agreement became public knowledge. Here was England having to deal with the Great Mogul, who was furious enough to halt trade–and the very person who had started it all was the man they had sent to prevent it!

Furthermore, Kidd hadn't returned with any bothersome pirates, just riches. Kidd's mission was obviously nothing more than a thinly veiled treasure hunt, political foes announced. The backers had to dissociate themselves from Captain Kidd to save their own careers. The very men who had been so anxious to befriend Kidd now wanted rid of him before any more political fallout occurred. Most important, their expedition leader had to be served up as a responsible party to placate India.

. . . . .

On May 8, 1701, William Kidd's trial began, but the prisoner was ill prepared for it. He had not been allowed to receive correspondence, have visitors, have pen and paper to

ABANDON HOPE, ALL YE WHO ENTER was the sentiment of London's horrendous Newgate Prison. Newgate was filled with the over–whelming stench of unbathed prisoners and general filth. It was also dark, damp, cold, over–crowded, filled with rodents, and as a result, disease ridden. It is said that prisoners were dunked in vinegar before they went to court in order to alleviate their stench.

take notes, or even have access to legal counsel until right before the trial started. And Kidd was quite sick from his two-year incarceration at Newgate. He had "great pain in the head and shaking." Worse still, his key evidence disputing the charge of piracy was the two passes, and they were missing. They could not be found among the papers forwarded by Bellomont, so they were either lost or never sent. Bellomont couldn't testify to their existence, assuming he would have, since he had died by that point.

As if things were not bad enough, Kidd was also charged with the murder of the mutinous gunman, William Moore. The allegation was substantiated by the testimony of two pirates who had deserted Kidd at Madagascar to join the pirate crew of Captain Culliford. They had been captured but had been offered freedom in exchange for giving damaging testimony against their former commander.

• • • • •

The trial lasted only two days. Here is the announcement:

The TRYAL of Capt. William Kidd

**for Murther & Piracy
Upon Six Several
Indictments
At the Admiralty
Sessions held at the OLD
BAILEY, London, on the
8th & 9th of May, 1701**

Captain William Kidd was found guilty of all crimes with which he had been charged: murder and five counts of piracy. His sentence was death. When the sentence was read, Kidd exclaimed, "My Lord, it is a very hard sentence. For my part, I am the innocentest person of them all, only I have been sworn against by perjured persons."

The two passes Kidd had relied on so heavily for his defense did turn up in a public records office in London almost two hundred years later! It's believed they were deliberately hidden so there would be no possibility of William Kidd's being found innocent.

His hanging was at a spot on the Thames River called Execution Dock. This area was chosen because it had the greatest amount of river traffic, so as to send a message that criminals, especially pirates, would not be tolerated. On May 23, 1701, William Kidd was led to the site of his impending death. It took two hours to get him through the crowd and up to the gallows. Someone in the crowd slipped him a bottle of liquor, which he gratefully consumed. Anxiously, the bystanders awaited a final speech that would include some kind of declaration of innocence or some pious words, but they were sorely disappointed.

Hordes of people typically showed up to watch pirate executions. Most longed to hear the final words of the sea robbers. These last words of pirates were printed and sold for a substantial amount of money.

Kidd gave no one such pleasure or source of income. He

did not speak. The noose was placed around his neck, but as his bad luck would have it, the rope broke and the man had to be rehanged. His body was later tarred for preservation and hung for many years as a reminder of what happens to those who go against the Crown. Shortly after Kidd's execution, war broke out between England and the Franco-American Alliance, so work as a privateer was once again plentiful. Piracy pretty much died out until the end of the war in 1713, which began the Golden Age of Piracy.

So, was Kidd really a pirate or a privateer who was a victim of old-fashioned politics, greed, a mutinous crew, and an impossible mission?

•   •   •   •   •

Kidd's treasure may not be as exaggerated as some believe. Four chests with four charts hidden in secret compartments of each have been discovered and are in the private collection of a man named Hubert Palmer. One of these chests, which was in Captain Kidd's cell, was stolen by a turnkey (guard) at Newgate Prison on the morning of Kidd's execution. These hidden charts are believed to be maps to Captain Kidd's buried treasure. However, because of some vague references and inaccuracies, such as "nameless island" and "Indies" (Does this refer to East or West Indies?), it seems Captain Kidd's treasure will never be fully recovered.

One story credits John Jacob Astor with obtaining one of Kidd's treasure chests. Supposedly, a chest was found in a cave in Deer Isle, Maine, in 1801 by a treasure hunter who was hired by Astor. However, this report is not widely believed to be true.

•   •   •   •   •

More About William Kidd

The *Adventure Galley* had 28,000 square feet of sail, composed of a woven blend of cotton, linen, and hemp. Although the ship was called the *Adventure Galley*, there was no galley (kitchen), only a basic wood-burning range.

. . . . .

After William Kidd's death, his wife, Sarah Kidd, remarried a man named Christopher Rousby. Her marriage license was granted on November 4, 1702, a little over five months after the death of Husband Number Three.

. . . . .

Samuel Bradley, who accompanied William Kidd on his venture, was his brother-in-law. When Kidd resorted to piracy to achieve his goals, Bradley was very much opposed to it. Known as the reluctant pirate, Samuel Bradley was marooned by Kidd on the Isle of St. Thomas, where Bradley soon died.

. . . . .

Edgar Allan Poe's "The Gold-Bug'" is a fictional story about Kidd's buried treasure on Sullivan's Island, South Carolina. The gist of the tale is that a young boy is sent to Charleston to spend the summer with his uncle. The boy discovers Sullivan's Island and begins spending time there in search of butterflies. He finds the island is not uninhabited, as he thought. A man and his mute servant are there in search of Captain Kidd's buried treasure. The men are determined to find the treasure, at any cost. The pair are forced to enlist the boy's help in order to do this, and the three become equal partners. Eventually, they do find the enormous treasure. The boy is sent back to the mainland to bring big sacks so they can load all their riches. By the time he returns, the two men are dead and the treasure is missing. It is believed Captain Kidd placed a curse on this treasure so that no one should find it and live to tell about it.

· · · · ·

Ballad of Captain Kidd

My name was William Kidd, when I sailed, when I sailed
My name was William Kidd, when I sailed
God's law I did forbid,
And so wickedly I did, when I sailed

My parents taught me well, when I sailed, when I sailed
My parents taught me well, when I sailed
to shun the gates of hell
But 'gainst them I rebelled, when I sailed

I'd a Bible in my hand, when I sailed, when I sailed
I'd a Bible in my hand,
By my father's great command,
And sunk it in the sand, when I sailed

I murdered William Moore, as I sailed, as I sailed
I murdered William Moore, as I sailed
I murdered William Moore,
And laid him in his gore,
Not many leagues from shore, as I sailed

I was sick and nigh to death, when I sailed, when I sailed
I was sick and nigh to death, when I sailed
I was sick and nigh to death

And I vowed at every breath
To walk in wisdom's ways, as I sailed
I thought I was undone, as I sailed, as I sailed
I thought I was undone, as I sailed
And my wicked glass hath run,
But health did soon return, as I sailed

My repentance lasted not, as I sailed, as I sailed
My repentance lasted not, as I sailed
My repentance lasted not
My vows I soon forgot
Damnation was my lot, as I sailed
I spyed the ships from France, as I sailed, as I sailed
I spyed the ships of France, as I sailed
I spyed the ships from France
To them I did advance
And took them all by chance, as I sailed

I spyed the ships of Spain, as I sailed, as I sailed
I spyed the ships of Spain, as I sailed
I spyed the ships of Spain,
I fired on them amain,
Till most of them was slain, as I sailed

I'd ninety bars of gold, as I sailed, as I sailed
I'd ninety bars of gold, as I sailed
I'd ninety bars of gold,
And dollars manifold,
With riches uncontrolled, as I sailed

Thus being o'ertaken at last, I must die, I must die
Thus being o'ertaken at last, I must die
Thus being o'ertaken at last,
And into prison cast
And sentence being past, I must die

Farewell, the raging main, I must die, I must die
Farewell, the raging main, I must die
Farewell, the raging main,
To Turkey, France and Spain
I shall ne'er see you again, I must die

To Execution Dock, I must go, I must go
To Execution Dock, I must go
To Execution Dock,
Will many thousands flock,
But I must bear the shock, and must die

Come all ye young and old, see me die, see me die
Come all ye young and old, see me die
Come all ye young and old,
You're welcome to my gold,
For by it I've lost my soul, and must die

Take warning now by me, for I must die, for I must die
Take warning now by me, for I must die
Take warning now by me,
And shun bad company,
Lest you come to hell with me, for I die

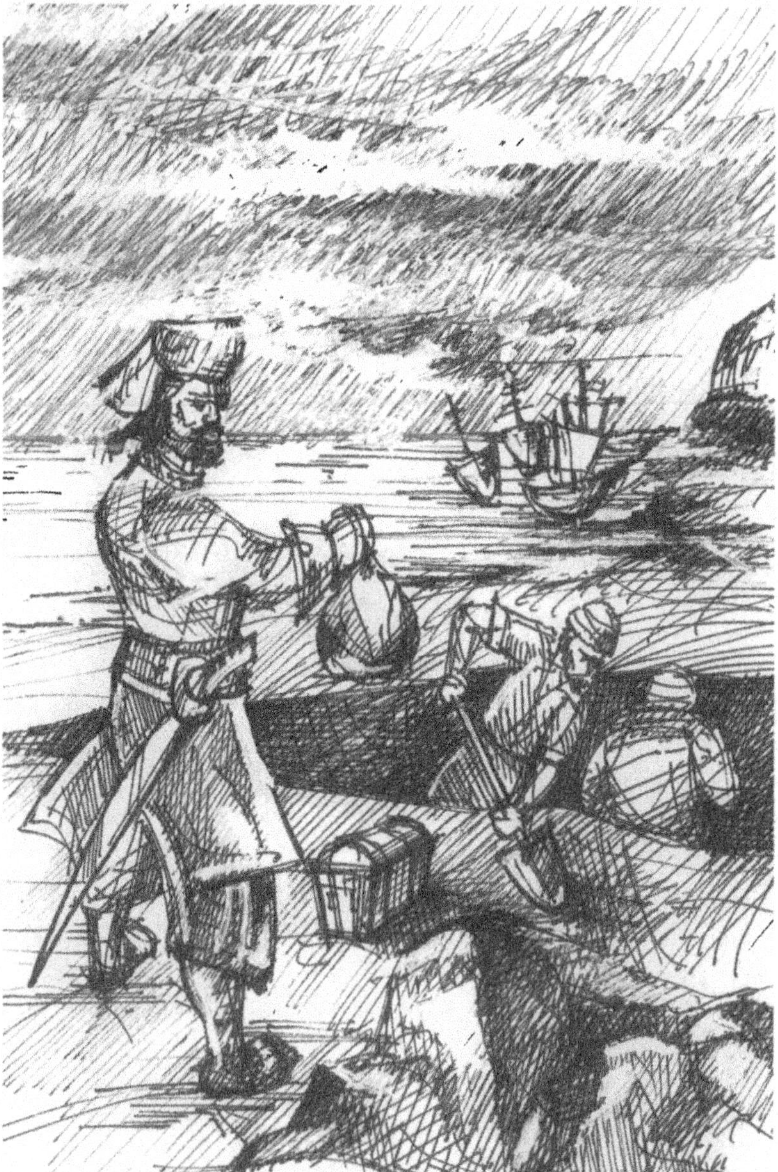

Julie Rabun

John Redfield

Redfield is memorable because of his connection to the infamous Captain Kidd and his legendary treasure.

Not much is known about John Redfield before he met up with the ill-famed Captain Kidd. It's believed he was a privateering captain during Queen Anne's War. What we do know for sure is that he was a devoted and trusted member of Kidd's crew.

As such, William Kidd made a strange request of him. Kidd did not want to return to New York with all his treasure for fear he would be arrested and the booty confiscated. The captain figured it would serve him well to stash some of the loot, either to use as a bargaining chip on his behalf, or for his own use once he was exonerated. However, he needed someone to keep an eye on it, and there was no one he trusted more than John Redfield.

· · · · ·

It's thought that Redfield was more than a loyal crew member–that he was an old friend of Kidd's. Certainly, he was one of the few men who had stayed loyal to Kidd throughout the lengthy journey, and he was also one of only a handful of men willing to return with the captain to clear his name. Once Kidd was assured he could count on him, he gave the dutiful man instructions. These are the alleged orders:

> I leave with you two chests. If I have not contacted you within the next five years, you may dig up one of the chests and help yourself to half its contents. If at the end of ten years time you have not heard from me, you may dig up the second chest and take half of its contents. I want you to remain in this area. Here is one thousand pounds for your participation.

That night they rowed over to a tiny island and buried the two chests. In a separate action, Redfield hid the money Kidd gave him for his participation. The next day they continued up the North Carolina coast, stopping near Albemarle Sound so that the pirate captain could round up a schooner and provisions for Redfield. Upon securing them, Kidd told four of his men they were now under Redfield's command.

William Kidd didn't know how these seamen would take to life on land, but he knew he could count on them to help build a house for Captain Redfield and get him settled. He dropped the group off and headed for New York. Whatever Kidd told his men about why they were to stay with Redfield, he didn't tell them about his buried treasure.

•   •   •   •   •

All the men had trouble adjusting to their new lifestyle. The area was very remote, and they quickly grew bored. They began taking day trips to the closest southern town, Charleston, South Carolina. It was a booming and bustling place, and they began to spend a great deal of time in this port town. His men found the chicanery they missed, and the lonely Redfield found a bride in Charleston.

Sometime during the spring of 1701, a vessel boasting Captain Kidd's colors (flag) arrived. As Redfield watched, a pirate and former crew member of Captain Kidd's, Max Brisbau, emerged. Redfield graciously but suspiciously invited him into his home. While having a drink, Brisbau explained he had been sent by Kidd to procure his buried treasure.

Although the pirate was persistent that he had been sent by Kidd, Redfield knew better. Max Brisbau did not give him the signal Captain Kidd had assured Redfield anyone he sent would use. Redfield's unwillingness to disclose the location of the chests made the pirate furious. Soon, both Redfield's and Brisbau's men returned to Redfield's house. The crews had met in Charleston and had decided to join forces, once Redfield's men were informed of the buried loot. The pirates assured Redfield he would get a good portion of the treasure, all he had to do was tell them where it was. Redfield refused. He shouted that he would never betray Captain Kidd.

The men looked for the booty without aid from Redfield but were unable to find it. Captain Brisbau devised a scheme to get the stubborn man to divulge once and for all where the treasure was hidden. He took Redfield and his wife aboard his ship by force and pulled up anchor. After the ship had been sailing for some time, Captain Brisbau turned to the tied-up couple and demanded, "Tell me where the treasure is or prepare to be thrown overboard! Now!"

Whether Redfield would have disclosed the location of the trunks will never be known. Also, whether Brisbau really would have freed the couple and split the treasure can't be answered. Before any action could be taken, the ship was detained when port authorities pulled up to the vessel and discovered it had prisoners aboard. When asked for papers proving Brisbau's claim that the vessel was nothing more than a merchant ship, the pirate captain was unable to comply. The vessel was seized, and all the pirates were jailed. Redfield and his wife gave testimony, which excluded any mention of the treasure story, and the couple was soon freed.

Not long after this, news of Captain Kidd's demise at Execution Dock reached Redfield. He was sorry to hear the grim story of his old friend and employer. The good news was that the buried booty was all his. The couple moved to Charleston and bought a big house. The community assumed Redfield had secured his immense wealth through shrewd business dealings. Wouldn't his peers have been shocked to learn that the money the couple possessed was linked to the disreputable Captain William Kidd!

Part II

Pirate Lore
and Resources

The Truth about Piracy

Pirates have been around almost since the beginning of time, from Ancient Greece with "peirates" plundering the Aegean Sea to the present. However, the biggest era of piracy was during the late seventeenth and early eighteenth centuries. This was known as the Golden Age of Piracy.

The single most important reason for this was that during Queen Anne's War between England and France, a huge navy—fifty thousand sailors at its peak—was necessary. After more than a decade of hostilities, the war ended in 1713 and the military was reduced to fifteen thousand. This left a heck of a lot of unemployed sailors. It also left many out-of-work privateers and captured slaves. These men turned to piracy in record numbers.

Another reason for the increase in piracy was the discovery of America, which led to its plunder by England, France, and Spain. Additionally, merchant ships increasingly sailed trade routes from Europe to the Caribbean.

Favorite pirate ports included Port Royal, Jamaica, Madagascar, and the Bahamas (formerly New Providence). For most of the 1600s, Port Royal was a sleazy, lawless place that suited pirates perfectly. Port Royal suffered an earthquake in 1692 that swallowed the city, engulfed two thousand people, and claimed millions of dollars in pirate treasure. Underwater excavations of the sunken city are ongoing in the hopes of recovering artifacts and possible pirate booty.

Madagascar was appealing to pirates because it had not been colonized by Europeans, meaning it was not under their authority. Quite to the contrary, the native people welcomed the pirates. No one seemed to care who they were or what crimes they had committed as long as they had money to spend. Just to err on the side of caution, the pirates built a fort on St. Mary's Island (northeast Madagascar) in case they ever needed to defend themselves.

Pirate treasure is also called booty, loot, plunder, goods, riches, and prize.

Piracy has not been abolished; it has simply shifted with the times. Nowadays, rather than arrive in three-masted sloops, pirates use high-speed boats or dinghies to surprise their victims. In addition to international merchant ships, yachts are often targeted. What is the usual loot? It runs the gamut from high-end items such as jewelry and watches, to cash, to items of little value such as spare engines and cameras.

The problem is significant enough that the International Maritime Bureau (IMB) was established in order to monitor piracy around the world. In recent years, it has reported the highest number of attacks in the Far East. Southeast Asia's Java Sea and South China Sea remain hotbeds of piratical activity.

It is interesting to note that the same way that pirates once ran up "false colors" to convince a merchant ship that they too were merchant ships flying under the same flag, pirates are now donning coast guard uniforms to fool cargo ships and yachts.

Last year, there were 335 pirate attacks worldwide. In some instances, the IMB merely warns maritime traffic to stay at least 50 nautical miles offshore. Other times, they advise maritime traffic to stay away from an area if at all possible or to exercise extreme caution. These pirates are armed with mortars and rocket-propelled grenades, making them very dangerous.

What is being done to combat this modern piracy? New technology is the key. An Inventus UAV (unmanned aerial

The origin of the word pirate goes back to the Greek word *peirates*, which means "one who attacks." Over the years, many nicknames have been created for pirates:

- rogue
- outlaw
- sea robber
- buccaneer
- sea dog
- corsair
- sea scoundrel
- picaroon
- freebooter
- sea villain
- swashbuckler
- sea marauder

vehicle) is a sophisticated reconnaissance system providing aerial surveillance in real time. Secure Ship is another important innovation. This is an electrical fence that encompasses the ship to prevent intruders from boarding it. The 9,000-volt pulse gives off a nasty (though nonlethal) shock to marauders while sounding a piercing alarm and activating floodlights. At the least, IMB recommends a good ship-tracking device. As of 2004, ships weighing over 500 gross registered tonnage (grt) must be equipped with an onboard security alert system. If the ship and crew are in peril, a message is dispatched to the appropriate authorities without detection.

How to Talk Like a Pirate

Aft Rear of the ship

Ahoy Hello

Ballast Ship stabilizer

Belay Shut up

Bilge 1. Foolish talk. 2. Lowest area of ship inside the hull along the keel, which fills with stagnant (rank or contaminated) water that is known as bilge or bilge water

Blimey Exclamation of surprise

Blockade To prevent a ship from reaching a port

Bowsprit Spar at ship's prow

Brethren of the Coast This is what pirates dubbed themselves, especially in the late 1600s, because they were a brotherhood or fraternal organization. As such, they had a Code of Conduct and looked out for each other (to some degree).

Caulk When oakum (rope fibers) and tar are used to waterproof a ship for seaworthiness

Chantey (also **shanty**) Sailor sea song

Crow's nest Small, partially-enclosed platform near the top of a mast, used for various purposes, such as keeping a lookout for enemy or merchant ships, land, etc.

Cutlass A short sword and favorite weapon of pirates

Davy Jones' locker Nickname for the bottom of the ocean

"Dead men tell no tales" Pirate saying as to why they don't like to leave witnesses

Doubloon Spanish gold coin. At different times, it was worth either 4 or 16 silver pesos, or "pieces of eight."

"Fair winds" Fond wishes for good luck at sea

Gibbet Public gallows (body cage) used to hang executed pirates

"Gangway" Get out of the way

"Godspeed" Another way of saying goodbye and good luck on your voyage

Go on the account To take up piracy

Grenade Small hand-thrown bomb used in battle

Grog Alcoholic beverage such as rum or ale

Grub Slang for food

Gun Small cannon

Fore or forward Front end of the ship

Flogging Punishment of disobedient crew member by publicly whipping or caning, which helped keep other crew members in their rightful place.

Hands Slang for crew, as in "All hands on deck!"

Handsomely Another way of saying hurry up or be quick about it

Haven Safe place to hide out and make ship repairs or just to party

Hijack Seize ship and cargo—modern day pirates are often called hijackers, but it means the same thing.

Hull Outer part or shell of a ship

Jolly Roger Pirate flag

Keel Timber board that extends across bottom of ship's hull

Keelhaul Punishment by dragging a disobedient crew member under the ship. This was the most severe form of punishment and therefore reserved for only the worst infractions. The victim of this punishment often came close to drowning and typically suffered nasty wounds from the barnacles attached to the bottom of the ship.

Knot 1. Speed (one nautical mile per hour) 2. Method of tying ropes

Landlubber Nonsailor or someone who doesn't tolerate open seas well. Stede Bonnet reportedly suffered from seasickness–landlubber!

Letters of Marque These were papers issued by a government during a war authorizing the bearer (privateer) to attack enemy ships on behalf of his government. Any loot obtained was split between the privateer, the crew, and the government that he was working for, in accordance with each agreement. Yes, privateers were nothing more than licensed pirates!

Logbook Daily account of shipboard activities and course

Maroon Punishment for a naughty crew member sometimes included marooning him on a desert island where he had a slim chance of survival and rescue.

Merchant ship Trading ship carrying goods that pirates wanted

"No quarter" This short phrase meant that surrendering was not an option, because no mercy would be shown regardless.

Piece of eight Silver coin worth one Spanish peso. Sometimes it was divided into eight pieces, hence the name.

Pillage To raid, rob, or plunder

Pirate round Roundtrip voyage from North America or Caribbean to West Africa and the Indian Ocean

Piragua Dugout canoe sometimes used by Caribbean pirates

Poop deck Highest deck at the aft end of a large ship. There are no poop decks on smaller ships.

Quarterdeck The aft part of the upper deck of a smaller ship

Port 1. Seaport 2. Left side of the ship (when facing toward prow)

Prahu Sleek boat used by Asian pirates

Prow The nose of the ship

Rig Masts and sails of a ship

Rigging Rope system for masts and sails of a ship

Rudder Moveable (hinged) board at back of a ship that is used for steering it

Sail ho What the lookout or any crew member says when he has spotted a ship (or at least its sail)

Scuppers Openings along the edges of a ship's deck, which allow water to run off into the sea rather than collecting below deck as bilge water

Scurvy Vitamin deficiency (lack of vitamin C) due to poor sea diet

Shipshape Everything looks good and all is well on board., as in "Everything is shipshape, Cap'n!"

Shiver me timbers Expression of surprise or fear

Splice the mainbrace Just another way of saying "Let's enjoy a cold drink."

Spyglass Looking glass or telescope

Starboard Right side of ship (when facing toward prow)

Weigh anchor To reel the anchor back up for leaving port

Pirate Movies

Boy, do we like our pirates! There have been more than a dozen movies based on Robert Louis Stevenson's fictional tale, *Treasure Island.*

Treasure Island (1912, silent) Addison Rothermel
Treasure Island (1918, silent) Francis Carpenter
Treasure Island (1920, silent) Shirley Mason
Treasure Island (1934) Wallace Beery, Jackie Cooper
Treasure Island (1950) Bobby Driscoll, Robert Newton
Long John Silver (also known as **Long John Silver's Return to Treasure Island** (1954) Robert Newton, Connie Gilchrist
Treasure Island (1972) Orson Welles
Treasure Island (1973, animated)
Treasure Island (1985) Melvil Poupand, Martin Landau
Return to Treasure Island (1985, Disney TV miniseries)
Treasure Island (1990, TV movie) Charlton Heston, Christian Bale
Muppet Treasure Island (1996) Tim Curry
Return to Treasure Island (1996, TV movie) Dean O'Gorman, Stig Eldred
Treasure Island (1997, animated)
Treasure Island (1999) Jack Palance
Treasure Planet (2002, animated)

But our obsession with pirates doesn't stop there. From comedies to dramas and silent films to animated movies, we just keep making 'em!

Abbott & Costello Meet Captain Kidd (1952) Bud Abbott, Lou Costello
Against All Flags (1952) Errol Flynn, Maureen O'Hara.

Anne of the Indies (1951) Jean Peters
The Black Pirate (1926, silent) Douglas Fairbanks
The Black Pirates (1954) Lon Chaney Jr.
The Black Swan (1942) Tyrone Powers, Maureen O'Hara
Blackbeard the Pirate (1952) Robert Newton
Blackbeard's Ghost (1968) Peter Ustinov, Dean Jones
The Boy & the Pirates (1960) Charles Herbert
Breed of the Sea (1926, silent) Ralph Ince
The Buccaneer (1938) Frederic March
The Buccaneer (1958) Yul Brynner
Buccaneer's Girl (1950) Frederick de Cordova
Captain Blood (1935) Errol Flynn
Captain Calamity (1936) Vince Barnett
Captain Kidd (1945) Charles Laughton, Randolph Scott
Captain Kidd & the Slave Girl (1954) Eva Gabor, Lew
  Landers
Captain Pirate (1952, sequel to *Captain Blood*) Louis Hayward
Caribbean (1952) John Payne, Sir Cedric Hardwicke
Clothes Make the Pirate (1925, silent) Leon Errol
Crimson Pirate (1952) Burt Lancaster
Cutthroat Island (1995) Gena Davis, Matthew Modine
Daphne and the Pirate (1916, silent)
The Devil Ship Pirates (1964) Christopher Lee
Double Crossbones (1951) Will Geer
The First Kiss (1928, silent) Gary Cooper, Fay Wray
Fortunes of Captain Blood (1950, remake of *Captain Blood*)
  Louis Hayward
Frenchman's Creek (1944) Nigel Bruce, Basil Rathbone
Frenchman's Creek (1998, TV movie) Anthony Delon
Golden Hawk (1952) Rhonda Fleming, Sterling Hayden
The Goonies (1985) Christopher Lloyd
High Wind in Jamaica (1965) Anthony Quinn
Hook (1991) Robin Williams, Dustin Hoffman
Island (1980) Michael Caine
The King's Pirate (1963, remake of *Against All Flags*) Doug
  McClure

Last of the Buccaneers (1950) Paul Henreid

Magic Island (1995) Zachery Ty Bryan

The Master of Ballantrae (1953) Errol Flynn

The Master of Ballantrae (1984) Timothy Dalton, Michael York

Matusalem I & II (1993 & 1997) Jean Pierre Bergeron

Morgan the Pirate (1961) Steve Reeves

Nate and Hayes (1983) Tommy Lee Jones, Michael O'Keefe

Old Ironsides (1926, silent) Wallace Beery

Peg of the Pirates (1918, silent) Peggy Hyland

Peter Pan (1924, silent) Betty Bronson, Ernest Torrance

Peter Pan (1953, animated)

Peter Pan (2003) Jason Isaacs

The Pirate (1948) Gene Kelly, Judy Garland

Pirate of the Black Hawk (1961) Bridgett Bardot

The Pirate Movie (1982) Kristy McNichol, Christopher Atkins

Pirates (1986) Walter Matthau

Pirates of the Caribbean (2003) Johnny Depp, Orlando Bloom

The Pirates of Penzance (1983) Kevin Kline, Angela Lansbury

Pirates of the Plain (1999) Tim Curry

Pirates of the Seven Seas (1965) Steve Reeves

Pirates of Tortuga (1961) Ken Scott, John Richardson

Pirates of Tripoli (1955) Paul Henreid, Patricia Medina

The Princess and the Pirate (1944) Bob Hope

Queen of the Pirates (1960) Massimo Serato, Gianna Maria Canale

Rage of the Buccaneers (1962) Ricardo Montalban, Vincent Price

Raiders of the Seven Seas (1953) Lon Chaney, Jr., Donna Reed

Return to Never Land (2002, animated)

Sea Devils (1953) Rock Hudson

Sea Hawk (1924, silent) Milton Sills

Sea Hawk (1940) Errol Flynn
Sea Hound (1947) Buster Crabbe
The Sea Wolf (2003) Thomas Ian Griffith.
Shipwrecked (1991) Gabriel Byrne
Son of Captain Blood (1962) Sean Flynn (Errol Flynn's son)
The Spanish Main (1945) Maureen O'Hara, Paul Henreid
Swashbuckler (1976) Robert Shaw, James Earl Jones
Swiss Family Robinson (1960) John Mills, Dorothy McGuire
Three Little Pirates (1946) Curly Howard, Larry Fine, Moe Howard (The Three Stooges)
Yankee Buccaneer (1952) Jeff Chandler and Scott Brady
Yankee Pasha (1954) Jeff Chandler, Rhonda Fleming
Yellowbeard (1983) Peter Cook, Peter Boyle

There have even been books written chronicling all the movies about pirates, such as *Pirates & Seafaring Swashbucklers on the Hollywood Screen* by James Robert Parish.

Considering the list of pirate movies, which I'm certain is not complete, I'm not about to attempt to list the catalog of pirate literature. I believe that they go back as far as the 1600s with *Buccaneers of America* (1684, London), *A General History of the Robberies and Murders of the Most Notorious Pyrates* (1724, London), *Pirates' Own Book* (1837, Boston) and, of course, *Treasure Island* by Robert Louis Stevenson (1883).

Buccaneer Bios
Top Twenty Most
Infamous Pirates

(Note: These buccaneers span several different periods of piracy. Notice that nine of the twenty have ties to the Carolinas.)

Henry "Long Ben" Avery (1685–circa 1728) was dubbed the "Arch Pirate" because of his successful attack of a Great Mogul ship.

John "Calico Jack" Rackham (circa early 1700s) was most famous for his relationship with female pirate Anne Bonny, and for refusing to fight during his last battle.

Captain William Kidd (circa 1645–1701) remains the most controversial pirate. Some argue he was an honest-to-goodness privateer while others swear he was nothing more than a scheming pirate. What is known is that his "business partners" turned their backs on him when he needed them most!

Jean Lafitte (circa early 1800s) was nothing more than a pirate who ran a successful smuggling operation in the New Orleans area until the War of 1812 when he helped America against the British.

Henry Morgan (circa 1635–1688) got into piracy when he was abducted from Bristol, England and forced into slavery in Barbados.

Classic Pirate Tune

Fifteen men on a dead man's chest
Yo-ho-ho and a bottle of rum

Drink and the Devil
Had done for the rest

Yo-ho-ho and a bottle of rum

Anne Bonny (circa early 1700s) was one of the fiercest female pirates, of which there were few. Anne was the daughter of a wealthy businessman who ran away from home before her arranged marriage was to take place.

Mary Read (circa early 1700s) was in the military and then later operated a tavern before being captured and forced into piracy. She soon found she liked it and was also quite good at it!

Bartholomew "Black Bart" Roberts (1682–1722) reportedly plundered close to four hundred ships during his career.

Thomas Tew (circa late 1600s) is one of a few pirates to successfully complete the Pirate Round, a circumnavigation of the world.

Charles Vane (circa early 1700s) was most famous for his capture of a Spanish galleon ship loaded with riches.

Sam "Black" Bellamy (circa early 1700s) is best known for his capture of the *Whydah*, a ship loaded with treasure.

Madame Chang (circa early 1800s) took over her husband's pirate flotilla upon his death and discovered that she was a better pirate than he was!

Eustace the "Black Monk" (circa early 1200s) was a European monk who turned pirate for unknown reasons. He was beheaded in his final battle.

Stede Bonnet (circa early 1700s) earned the nickname "Gentleman Pirate" because he was the only gentleman to take up piracy and buy his own ship.

Francis Drake (circa 1540–1596) was master of all trades–a sailor, explorer, navigator, privateer, and pirate.

Peter Easton (circa early 1600s) was captain of a large flotilla that sailed around the world before the French government gave him the title Marquis Easton.

Victor Hugues (circa late 1700s) ran a slave trade business before turning to piracy.

Blackbeard (circa early 1700s) was one of the most successful pirates of all time. Some of his most infamous exploits include holding the City of Charles Town (Charleston, SC) hostage to get medical supplies he needed and defeating the Royal Navy on at least one occasion.

Simon "Captain Devil" Danziger (circa early 1600s) was a successful privateer who later turned pirate.

Christopher Condent (circa early 1700s) was an English pirate who plundered the waters from the Bahamas to Madagascar.

Pirate Quiz

Take this quiz to test your knowledge of piracy. You'll find the answers on page 162 (but don't peek).

1. 'Junks' were large sailing ships used by Chinese pirates.
    True or False

2. Long John Silver led twenty-two successful assaults during the Golden Age of Piracy.
    True or False

3. One of the greatest pirate-related productions was *The Pirates of Penzance.*
    True or False

4. Port Royal, Jamaica was a favorite haven for bucca-neers during the 1600s.
    True or False

5. Blackbeard got his nickname because he always wore black clothes.
    True or False

6. Navigating the high seas was a tricky business. Seamen, including pirates, relied on compasses, charts (maps), logbooks, capstans, backstaffs, spyglasses, and dividers. Which one of these terms does not belong here?

7. Scurvy was a big problem for pirates.
    True or False

8. Pirates had a Code of Conduct.
    True or False

9. Pirate executions had large turnouts. Crowds came and cheered, as if it were prime entertainment. The largest crowd, however, was at Stede Bonnet's hanging.
    True or False

10. Who made one of the biggest fortunes in pirate history and yet died a pauper?

11. Pirates sometimes painted over their gun ports.
    True or False

12. What is careening?

13. Did pirates really put parrots on their shoulders, or is that a myth?

14. What was some good booty (treasure)?

15. Did pirates normally bury their treasure?

16. The most popular name for a pirate ship was *Adventure*.
    True or False

17. Did pirates have wooden legs?

18. Where and how did pirates sleep?

19. There were four types of pirate flags.
    True or false

20. What did pirates do when they were on land?

21. What did pirates typically eat?

22. Did they really hang pirates?

23. What was the average life expectancy of a pirate?

24. When a pirate was marooned, he was left on an island with nothing but the clothes on his back.
    True or False

25. Did pirates really make victims and mutinous crew members walk the plank?

26. Piracy still exists in modern times.
    True or False

Pirate Ships

Victory in battle always comes down to strategy and firepower, and pirates were no different. Their plan of action and weapons available to carry out this plan were crucial to their success.

The most important weapon of a pirate captain was his ship. There were two sizes of vessels. A pirate chose a large **three-masted vessel** if he was taking on merchant ships on the open seas. The big ship was loaded with roughly forty guns and served to intimidate the intended victim into immediate surrender.

The smaller ships were for inland pirates such as Blackbeard, once he left the high seas and took to sailing around the sounds and inlets of the Carolinas. These ships had a single mast. These **sloops, schooners,** or **brigantines** were made for speed and maneuverability.

The sloop was the smallest, weighing in at under 100 tons. Her strengths were speed and ease of control. The ship could accommodate about a dozen cannons and fifty or so pirates. The schooner weighed about the same as a sloop but had a different design, making it sturdier but not as fast. Because it was slightly bigger and heavier, it could hold more pirates, cannons, and swivel guns. The brigantine was the biggest of this group. It weighed more than 150 tons and could safely hold about one hundred pirates and around twelve cannons. This was the best ship of these three if you might have to do battle.

Pirate Weapons

Boarding ax Like a regular-size ax, only heavier. It was used to slash sails, cut through wood, smash skulls, break down doors, etc.

Cutlass A short, heavy sword that curves slightly at its tip for optimum slashing

Dagger A big knife with a thicker blade than a normal knife or a dirk (small dagger)

Grappling irons Metal hooks used to board an enemy ship

Grenade A small bomb thrown onto enemy ship before boarding

Guns or pistols Seventeenth century pistols and guns could fire off only one bullet. There were no chambers to hold additional bullets. Therefore, most pirates had holsters laden down with as many as six guns.

> *Types of guns and rifles*
> Blunderbuss (equal to the musketoon)
> Flintlock (popular pirate gun)
> Musket (single shot rifle)
> Musketoon (lesser version of the musket)
> Powderhorn (a pouch or box that held gunpowder)

Soap or grease Used to make a deck slippery. If your enemy jumped aboard your ship and his feet shot out from underneath him, you had the upper hand!

Spears were sometimes used to lessen the number of opponents before jumping on board for hand-to-hand combat.

Swivel (swing) guns Small cannons that could pitch a 70-pound ball a distance of up to half a mile. A fast gunner could clean and reload in under four minutes.

Tacks were spread out on a ship's deck to cut the feet of those who jumped aboard. (Note: Most Caribbean sailors didn't wear heavy shoes at that time, if they wore shoes at all.)

Quiz Answers

1. *True.* Masterful pirate Cui Apu had five hundred junks under his command in the South China Sea until his death in 1851.

2. *False.* Long John Silver was a fictional character in Robert Louis Stevenson's *Treasure Island*.

3. *True.* While many entertaining movies and productions have been staged about pirates, this amusing opera is one of the best.

4. *True.* Port Royal had few laws and was host to drunken sailors, slave traders, gamblers, and pirates. That is, until June 7, 1692 when a freak earthquake annihilated the entire town.

5. *False.* Blackbeard, also dubbed the "Black-faced Devil" and "Fury from Hell" got his name because he was tall, dark, and had long black hair and a black beard, which he braided to create a more shocking appearance. To further confuse opponents, he tied lit fuses under his hat before going into battle so there was a smoky haze around his head.

6. *Capstans.* The capstan is a part of the ship, not a navigational tool. Pirates were not much for record keeping, but when used properly, logbooks showed a ship's speed, which could then be used to compute distance traveled. It also recorded pertinent information about the crew and voyage. A backstaff is used to find the ship's position in relation to the sun–the navigator turns his back to the sun and measures its shadow. A divider is used to measure distances on a map. A spyglass is used to note landmasses and other ships. A compass reveals whether a ship is sailing north, south, east, and/or west.

7. *True.* In the mid–1750s, it was discovered that consuming fresh fruit and vegetables could ward off this disease, so pirates began adding a lemon wedge or lime slice to their rum and ale.

8. *True.* Interestingly, there were certain fundamental rules of piracy. These varied from captain to captain, and some were stricter than others. Common rules included payment for loss of a limb or eye during battle, and no fighting each other aboard ship.

9. *False.* The largest turnout for a pirate execution was for Captain Kidd. His body was tarred and placed into a gibbet so that no one (such as his family or friends) could steal the body for a proper burial . The execution was held at the Execution Dock on the Thames River in London in 1701.

10. Henry "Long Ben" Avery. His "riches to rags" story is absolutely fascinating.

11. *True.* This was a technique used sometimes to fool merchant ships into thinking that they, too, were merchant ships.

12. Careening was when a ship was turned on its side so that its underside could be cleaned of damaging barnacles and worms, and/or have such damage repaired. Both impeded speed and seaworthiness over time. Pirates needed safe havens to accomplish this because they were vulnerable to attacks and capture during this time.

13. Yes! Parrots were a popular pirate souvenir from exotic trips (and much easier to manage than monkeys). Parrots were valuable in London bird markets and also as bribes to British naval officers.

14. So many possibilities: Spanish gold doubloons (one doubloon was worth seven weeks pay for a pirate crew,

on average), pieces-of-eight (Spanish pesos), any kind of weapons, gunpowder, medicine of any kind, any alcoholic beverage, gold or copper snuffboxes, fine fabrics (such as silk and linen), any food (especially meat, sugar, and flour), jewelry, or anything that could be sold or bartered.

15. No! Pirates didn't worry about planning for tomorrow. They usually didn't live long enough to be concerned with retirement accounts. The only time they buried their treasure was when they were afraid they might be caught and didn't want evidence of their crime. Or, in Captain Kidd's case, he hid his treasure to have leverage with the authorities once he found out he was a wanted man.

16. *False. Revenge* was the most commonly used name for a pirate ship.

17. Yes! Pirates were frequently injured during battle or shipboard accidents. The solution back then was to cut off the leg (or arm, which answers the question about whether they really had hooks, as well).

18. Sleeping accommodations were poor, to say the least. The pirate captain and a few officers had cabins at the stern. Those on duty stayed up all night keeping watch, while the rest of the crew slept communally below deck. The area stank due to bilge water (remember that this is the stagnant water that collects in the lowest part of the ship), rats roamed freely, and the boat pitched and rocked throughout the night, even if anchored.

19. *False.* There were two types of pirate flags. One was a red flag ("Red Jack") and it served as a warning to surrender and no one would be harmed. The red represented the bloodshed that would occur if victims didn't cooperate. The other type of flag was a black flag ("Jolly Roger"). The word "roger" was English slang for rogue or rover. The

Jolly Roger flag meant that death, represented by the color black, was imminent. This flag meant sure death to anyone who put up a fight. The pictures on the flags varied because they were symbols of each pirate. There were, however, standard icons used: crossed bones, skulls, skeletons, and cutlasses. Notice a theme?

20. Just what you might expect. They drank. They listened to music performed by crew members or locals. They danced. They played cards. They chased women. They slept. "Mock trials" were favorite amusements. Each man assumed a different role: judge, defendant, juror, etc. The judge jokingly handed down sentences. This game served two purposes. First, it reminded the men what could happen to them if they were caught. More importantly, it kept them in practice as to what to say and how to behave if they were apprehended.

21. Anything they could get their hands on! They were not picky eaters. The most popular pirate foods were turtles (and turtle eggs), fish, wild boar and pig, birds, hens (and hen eggs), hardtack (biscuits made of flour and water), and soup or stew. Wine, rum, and ale were popular beverages.

22. Absolutely! It served to discourage piracy and was a form of entertainment. Big crowds turned out to watch the execution and everyone was highly interested in a pirate's last words. Good money was paid to document the final sentences spoken before a pirate's execution. Gibbet cages were custom-made to fit a pirate's body. The blacksmith made it tight fitting so that the bones remained in the cage even after the flesh had rotted away. Even though the bodies were usually dipped in tar to preserve them for lengthy viewing, eventually the body decomposed.

The purpose of the cage was two-fold. First, it served to remind everyone how it inevitably ended for those who took up piracy–that is why the bodies were placed in prominent places, such as along the Thames River in London or in the Charleston harbor. Second, the heavy iron cage prevented relatives from stealing the bodies for burial.

23. Not long! One out of three pirates never made it back from sea, usually dying from a battle wound or disease. It was nearly impossible to prevent infection from occurring once wounded and there was rarely adequate medicine available to combat whatever ailed you. Pirate diets were lacking in vitamins, minerals, and proteins. However, by the mid–1700s it was discovered that eating fresh fruit or vegetables could prevent some diseases, such as scurvy. So pirates began adding an orange wedge or a lime slice to their grog. I guess we have the pirates to thank for the invention of fruit cocktails!

24. *True* in some cases, but not often. The marooning procedure varied with every captain. Some gave a tiny ration of food and water and some left the stranded pirate with only a knife or a pistol loaded with one bullet.

25. No! Pirates usually killed only those who stood in their way of treasure. Otherwise, they were left unharmed more often than not. Punishment for mutinous crew was to maroon them. It is rumored, however, that Henry Avery threw passengers overboard as he tired of feeding them when he seized a ship belonging to the Great Mogul.

26. *True.* Privateering and piracy lasting more than five thousand years but came to an end in the early nineteenth century when most countries signed the Treaty of Paris. This ended Letters of Marque (authorization) to privateers. The advancement of shipbuilding and military power also contributed to the end of piracy. Or did it? While shipbuilding technology and military prowess has advanced, so have the techniques and determination of modern–day pirates. Piracy remains a significant problem worldwide.

Scoring

19 out of 25 correct answers = You are ready to command your own ship.

11 – 18 correct answers = You show promise, but you spend too much time drinking grog!

5 –10 correct answers = Put down the grog, matey!

0 – 4 correct answers = Not even Blackbeard can make you a pirate!

Museums

There are many great maritime museums throughout the world. For more information, contact The National Maritime Museum Association, Building 35, Fort Mason, San Francisco, CA 94147; 415-561-NMMA(6662); www.maritime.org; www.maritimemuseums.net is a helpful resource for finding locations, online maritime sites, and other related information.

North Carolina Maritime Museum
315 Front Street
Beaufort, NC 28516
252-728-7317
www.ah.dcr.state.nc.us/
    sections/maritime

Graveyard of the Atlantic Museum
Hatteras-Ocracoke Ferry
    Terminal and U.S. Coast
    Guard Base
Hatteras Island, NC
252-986-2995
www.graveyardoftheatlantic.
    com

The Hall of American Maritime Enterprise
National Museum of
    American History
Smithsonian Institution
Washington, DC 20560
202-357-2025
www.si.edu

Hawaii Maritime Center
Pier 7
Honolulu, HI 96813
808-523-6151
www.bishopmuseum.org

Jean Lafitte Tourist Commission
2654 Jean Lafitte Blvd.
 Lafitte, LA 70067
(less than 30 minutes from
    New Orleans)
800-689-3525
www.jeanlafittetours.com
*There are lots of interactive exhibits
    and special displays, including
    one of the final battle of Jean
    Lafitte.*

The Mariners' Museum
100 Museum Drive
Newport News, Virginia
    23606
757-595-2222
www.mariner.org

Mystic Seaport Museum

75 Greenmanville Avenue
Mystic, CT 06355
860-572-5339
www.mystic.org

National Maritime Museum

Greenwich, London (England)
+44 (0) 20 8858 4422
www.nmm.ac.uk
This is the largest maritime museum in the world. It features more than two million maritime-related objects.

New England Pirate Museum

274 Derby Street
Salem, MA 01970
(Across from Pickering Wharf)
978-741-2800
www.piratemuseum.org

Patriots Point Naval and Maritime Museum

40 Patriots Point Road
Mt. Pleasant, SC 29464
www.patriotspoint.org
This is the largest museum of its kind in the world, featuring warships, aircraft carriers, and much more.

Peabody Essex Museum

East India Square
Salem, MA 01970
978-745-9500 or
    800-745-4054
www.pem.org

Pilgrim Monument and Provincetown Museum

Cape Cod
Provincetown, MA
www.pilgrim-monument.org
"Treasures of the Whydah" is on permanent display. The single biggest pirate treasure ever retrieved belonged to Sam Bellamy. The buccaneer captured an English trading ship, the Whydah, and subsequently lost it in a storm in off Cape Cod in 1717. It remained there until it was discovered in 1983 by Barry Clifford, who with Paul Perry, wrote a book about his quest, Expedition Whydah: The Story of the World's First Excavation of a Pirate Treasure Ship and the Man Who Found Her.

The Pirates of Nassau Museum

At the waterfront near Straw-market
Nassau, Bahamas
This is an interactive pirate museum that opened in late 1998. For more information or to send free pirate postcards electronically, log onto their website: www.pirates-of-nassau.com

Pirate Soul Museum

524 Front Street
Key West, FL 33040
305-292-1113
www.piratesoul.com

*The 5,000-square-foot museum
features more than 500 artifacts
from the golden age of piracy, as
well as numerous interactive
exhibits.*

South Street Seaport Museum

207 Front Street
New York, NY 10038
212-669-9400
www.southstseaport.org

Treasure Island Museum

Building One
Treasure Island
San Francisco, CA 94130
415-395-5067
www.treasureislandmuseum.org

Pirate Museum

Across from Pickering Wharf
274 Derby Street
Salem, MA 01970
978-741-2800

*This is a small museum, but worth
your while. The guide leads you
through a mock cave lined with
pirate exhibits, such as several
pirates below deck of their ship
and pirates enjoying an evening
at port in a tavern.*

Resources

There are so many books on piracy that it is hard to know where to begin, but here are a few of my favorite references.

Botting, Douglas. *The Seafarers: The Pirates*. Alexandria, VA: Time-Life Books, 1978.

Cordingly, David. *Under the Black Flag*. New York: Random House, 1995.

Cordingly, David and John Falconer. *Pirates: Fact and Fiction*. London: Collins & Brown Ltd., 1992.

Ellms, Charles. *The Pirates*. Avenel, NJ: Gramercy Books, 1996.
    This book was originally published in 1837 under the title *The Pirates' Own Book*.

Johnson, Charles. *A General History of the Robberies and Murders of the Most Notorious Pirates*. New York: The Lyons Press, 1998.
    This book was originally published in 1724.

Lee, Robert E. *Blackbeard the Pirate: A Reappraisal of His Life and Times*. Winston-Salem, NC: John F. Blair Publishing Co., 1995.

Moore, David D. "A General History of Blackbeard the Pirate, the Queen Anne's Revenge and the Adventure." *Tributaries*, v. 7 (1997): 31–35.

Norris, Allen Hart. *Beaufort County, North Carolina Deed Book I, 1696–1729: Records of Bath County, North Carolina*. Washington, NC: Beaufort County Genealogical Society, 2003.

Platt, Richard. *Eyewitness Books: Pirates*. New York: Alfred A. Knopf, 1994.

Rankin, Hugh F. *Pirates of Colonial North Carolina*, Eighth Edition. Raleigh, NC: Dept. of Cultural Resources, Division of Archives and History, 1979.

Reinhardt, David. *Pirates and Piracy*. New York: Konecky & Konecky, 1997.

Steele, Philip. *Pirates*. New York: Kingfisher, 1997.

Index

Other Titles by Terrance Zepke

Best Ghost Tales of North Carolina and *Best Ghost Tales of South Carolina*. The actors of Carolina's past linger among the living in these thrilling collections of ghost tales. Experience the chilling encounters told by the winners of the North Carolina "Ghost Watch" contest. Use Zepke's tips to conduct your own ghost hunt.

Coastal North Carolina, Second Edition. Terrance Zepke visits the Outer Banks and the upper and lower coasts to bring you the history and heritage of coastal communities, main sites and attractions, sports and outdoor activities, lore and traditions, and even fun ways to test your knowledge of this unique region. Includes more than 50 photos.

Coastal South Carolina. Terrance Zepke shows you historic sites, pieces of history, recreational activities, and traditions of the South Carolina coast. Includes recent and historical photos.

Ghosts and Legends of the Carolina Coasts. This collection of 28 stories ranges from hair-raising tales of horror to fascinating legends from the folklore of North and South Carolina. Learn about the eerie Fire Ship of New Bern and meet the dreaded Boo Hag.

Ghosts of the Carolina Coasts. Taken from real-life occurrences and Carolina Lowcountry lore, these 32 spine-tingling ghost stories take place in prominent historic structures of the region.

Ghosts of the Carolinas for Kids. Be careful in the Carolinas! Do you hear music, whispers, screams, moans, banging, footsteps, tapping, or thumping? Have the lights been turning on and off? Has the door opened and closed by itself? Discover what the Gray Man warns people about and which ghost leaves pennies for the homeowners. Ages 9 and up.

Lighthouses of the Carolinas, Second Edition. Here is the story of each of the 18 lighthouses that aid mariners traveling the coasts of North and South Carolina. Includes visiting information and photos.

Lighthouses of the Carolinas for Kids. A colorful and fun book filled with the history and lore of the lighthouses guarding the Carolina coasts, from Currituck at the top to Haig Point at the bottom. Meet some of the keepers who braved storms and suffered loneliness. Learn how lighthouses operated in the early days and how they work now. Ages 9 and up.

Lowcountry Voodoo: Beginner's Guide to Tales, Spells and Boo Hags. A compilation of some of the beliefs, special spells, and remarkable stories passed down through generations of Gullah families who have made their home in the South Carolina and Georgia Lowcountry.

Pirates of the Carolinas for Kids. The Carolinas had more than their share of pirates, including Calico Jack, Billy Lewis, Long Ben Avery, and two women, Anne Bonny and Mary Read. Ages 9 and up.

For more information on Terrance Zepke's books and future projects, visit her at
www.terrancezepke.com.

CPSIA information can be obtained
at www.ICGtesting.com
Printed in the USA
BVOW03s0314200117
474023BV00001B/1/P

9 781561 643448

CPSIA information can be obtained
at www.ICGtesting.com
Printed in the USA
LVHW02s1729260718
585040LV00002B/265/P